LETTERS

from JANE

*The Adventures of an
Abandoned Kitten*

BARBARA ALLAN HITE
drawings by Rick Hite

Trafford
PUBLISHING®

ISBN: 978-1-4269-4884-8 (sc)
ISBN: 978-1-4269-4885-5 (e)

Trafford rev. 03/02/2011

 www.trafford.com

North America & international
toll-free: 1 888 232 4444 (USA & Canada)
phone: 250 383 6864 ♦ fax: 812 355 4082

FOR THE TRIBE

One continues to love and thank all those who lived and played so long on Baldwin Avenue, and with Margaret and Fletch at the Oaks, in the Oak Grove and, of course, at Pennyroyal Farm, in its tool shed and environs. Who can fully say where those places have taken us, if we can think of being in a place that is going somewhere? Theater Wagon! To moments of love and creativity that brought us to life, on the stage or singing in one voice or talking all night. Can we think of where we'd be if we hadn't found, been led to or stumbled upon them?

No wonder we come back over and over again.

REFLECTION

Prior to the untimely death of our mother, we were four; now we are three, and yes, we are blind. What we have always done is to remember to sniff all the more frequently, to listen all the more carefully and to travel along well-worn paths close to the sides of walls and the edges of steps. We do, all three of us, fully acknowledge the extent to which accident and luck direct our lives, no matter what our physical circumstances, and so, yes, we have recently concluded that our congenital defect had little, if anything, to do with the loss of our tails.

Transcripts of Animal Trials by Bennett Wilson

LETTERS from Jane

PREAMBLE

Edited by the illustrious Edith Throckmorton, these coming-of-age epistles reveal predicaments of street dwelling creatures little known to the sheltered reader, encounters ranging from raccoon to gerbil, with both predictable and unpredictable outcomes. The letters, woven together in a narrative by the kitten Jane's best friend, Danny Lunder, tell of her early life in two different family situations and of the adjustments she was required to make when, due to no fault of her own, she was sent out into the homeless world at a still very young age.

PREFACE

Inexperienced as I was in the use of the Dog and Cat languages, my first inclination was to say "thank you, but no," to the request that I help edit a bundle of scruffy-looking papers—letters, as it turned out—written by a cat and submitted to me by a dog. As I first saw them, these letters lay in a crumpled pile on a polished kitchen floor; and as spotlighted by a stream of filtered window light, they appeared dingy, even dirty in those surroundings and unpromising to say the least, but there they lay, somehow calling to me on that sunny spring day—yes, a sunny spring day that was to change my life, a day that now seems many years ago but was, in fact, most likely only one year ago, my time.

I first met the Labrador Retriever by accident; this is the dog that the household here calls Tyler but whose first (original or real) name was Danny Lunder. The accident was mine. I had left the library bookcase one evening much earlier than my usual time; the clock must have said, oh, something like 12:30 or 1:00 (p.m., of course). When I arrived in the kitchen to see what was "leftoverandout," as we scavengers say, I moved like a slug under a flower pot. The dog was a new one to me; I had seen it only once or twice, and that from afar. There it was lying beside what looked to be a recently re-licked food bowl. Imagine my surprise when it indicated the bowl and began pushing it toward me with its nose, drooling and snuffling along the way. Now, to the naked, as they say, eye (naked eye referring to what I assume to be the open and wide-awake human eye, for who else is concerned in any particular scientific way about kitchen sanitation), to that eye, there was nothing at all edible to be seen in the dog's bowl, and the so-called average human being, I imagine, would be terrified to know that my hunger was completely and deliciously satisfied by the unseen grease and kibble particles left on the sides of that empty bowl, and what's more, that I, in fact, could live for a year or longer on the naked body of the human himself so long as he didn't wash his hair too frequently.

The sort of generosity involved in the dog's open sharing of what was probably his only meal of that day was surprising to me, but even more surprising was the way that dog backed out of the room as I began eating. In fact, his movement led me to spring up and over to the outside edge of the food bowl, then to hover near the floor, then to creep up to the top again, then to see him reenter very shortly with a mouth full of creamy and brownish, we could say, antique-shaded, crinkled and torn sheets of paper, incredibly messy, of various sorts—paper napkins, envelopes, and the like—which he put down, as if it were an offering, in front of me. Well, I like a mouthful of envelope adhesive now and again, but these pages revealed no edible residue of any kind at all. Then, if I must make a long story short, the dog explained in broken Roach that he wanted someone, me, to help him edit the writing on the papers, which I could see was Cat, to translate it, and to construct a connective narrative to hold the whole thing together. In short, again, he intended, with my help, to have these letters typed up in book form and submitted, somewhere (and who knew then if he had any idea of what that would involve) for publication.

Well. Well. The request suggested a tremendous mouthful of opportunity for me, unpublished as I was at that time, but the work to be done also promised to be tremendous. I am well versed in literary traditions, of course, being descended from a long and illustrious line of roach writers, but for this project, I would have to brush up both my Dog and my Cat and I would need to learn a wide array of new technical skills, not the least of which would be mastering the latest writing machine foisted upon us (that one called a "computer") and learn to deal with its one largest inconvenience—namely, a lack of escape space between keys. (I loved those old Royals with their bold, free-standing letters and their uncovered, cavernous insides.) But, as is obvious to see, I have done what needed to be done, although not always without "glitches" (note the use of new technological word) and not always with complete good will, for I can plainly see how all this advanced communicative technology, this digital god, as it is, here and everywhere, will plow its way into the meadows of our thoughts, so eager to help us work faster and clearer that it digs out and makes compost of all our complexities, reducing our languages to long weedy vines of flowerless banality. I, myself, have worked with only a bit of charcoal for most of my life, believing (in my inexperienced way) that if it was good enough for the Paleolithic composer, it ought to be good enough for me.

But what a challenge! I will use this politically correct word to avoid the negative connotations of the word "problem." I like a challenge. I'm not opposed to returning favors either; I was and continue to be grateful to the dog for that food bowl every night of my recent life. And so, again, to shorten what could be a fascinating but lengthy story, let me just say that I accepted Danny Lunder's offer. What you will see before you, if you look, is the fruit of much labor, gently pressing the pomegranates of life into liquid before our very eyes, his and mine, during what must have been more than a year's time to bring this project to life. You will have to be the judge, Dear Reader, in determining whether our efforts have been successful, but I am delighted to report that we have received two movie offers thus far, and we have not yet even found a publisher! This is some strange affair, to be sure, and to think that such much appreciated encouragement came to us long before the "clubs" announced their choices or the book-signing tours their schedules.

So, all has gone even better than planned up to this point. Yes, and I can highly recommend you read on. Here's to a dark, mysterious midnight and a pile of what looked like trash! Ah. And well I do remember a sunny, spring afternoon, also...or was it dusk... Never mind. Here's to complexity and confusion along with anything else that comes along! Let us contemplate: ART! And so, as we now say—in anticipation of a chocolate mint as well as a Beethoven sonata—enjoy!

E. Throckmorton

BIOGRAPHICAL NOTES FOR EDITH THROCKMORTON

Born within the last three months of this writing, Edith Throckmorton was raised under the sink in a fully operative modern kitchen facility, where she was designated by the woman of the establishment to be a member of the common cockroach family (scientific name, *Blattaria domesticus* or, perhaps, *Periplanata americana*). The fact is that she belongs to a more unusual genus, one that is rumored to be, if any household resident were interested in circulating rumors about it, of Asian descent. Although referred to as a "waterbug" in some necks of the woods, this insect should always be designated by its correct name, *Blatta orientalis*, for it is an insect that is blacker, larger, and (Ms Throckmorton would insist) "cleaner" than any common roach.

Roaches of various genetic lines and backgrounds have contributed prodigiously to the literary world, the most well known, perhaps, being the Archy writer of the Archy and Mehitabel materials; Archy claimed he was a poet reincarnated as a cockroach. Of course, we may never know how many poets are writing as roaches today, given the prejudice and health concerns of the times, but it is certain that, as Archy so aptly put it, they do look at things from the "underside."

The name Edith was attached to Throckmorton as a continuation of a *Blatta* family tradition, which was always to give a certain female of the 200,000 or so surviving in the household each year a literary name and one that she would grow into. Countless Throckmorton females (some using pseudonyms) have been a part of Eastern and Western literary traditions going back to prehistory, although, because of their unassuming natures, we do not know how many embodied which souls of which poets. In the tradition, however, it was deemed fitting to bestow upon at least one female infant from each year's hatchlings a name equal in length to that which she, as the truly talented, survival-oriented literary adult, should grow into. She could be larger, but no smaller than a given name of five characters added to the surname Throckmorton. Naturally, size, like time, can seem inexplicably relative, however, and it took years of calculation and debate before the details were ironed out. Now, we can safely say that the name length sets out as Times New Roman, 12 point font (caps, of course) as:

EDITHTHROCKMORTON

This is a large font to fill, but fill it she did! With family encouragement and bountiful table scraps, she reached from E to N in two months after hatching. When she moved into the library at an early age, Ms. Throckmorton became proficient in the grammar, linguistics, and literary criticism of five mammalian languages in addition to her own Insect and its variations. Naturally, she would never have referred to *herself* as a poet in any sense of the word, for she was a stickler for clarity and accuracy. These skills and more she brought to the project suggested by the Labrador Retriever she met in the summer of what was then six months ago. Thus began a collaboration that resulted in the production of this small, but effectively unique, volume, and led, in the end, to a situation that altered both their lives.

The Editor/Publisher

BOOK ONE

Part 1

In which the narrator, Danny Lunder, describes how he discovered the letters, and in which the first few letters themselves give an honest and intimate description of how one can become left and unwanted on the street:

It was colder than usual. It had been cold for two weeks dog time, but in the last two days, it was worse; the ice made walking painful, and the Master kept the walks too short then. At night, the Master took him around the block only once and did not stop at the playground by the school. Danny Lunder missed using the back anchor poles of the soccer goal and a spot beside the first rung of the sliding board. Jane tried to come along sometimes, but she hated the cold on her feet, and anyway, it was hard for them to concentrate on a conversation with the Master there. So, they felt lost from each other even before they finally were.

He knew Jane was hungry that whole time. She was a small cat, but even so, the small amount of food he tried to bring to her wouldn't stay in his mouth long enough for him to get it to the door, much less out onto the back porch. He didn't know why the Master had put her outside at that time but suspected it was because of Maisie—Maisie that ... (he was about to say "bitch" when he caught himself. "Wrong species but right concept," he thought. Well, "cuff,

cuff.") When he read the letters, he saw he was right about Maisie, at least in part.

> (*As must be obvious to any discerning Reader, Danny Lunder is inexperienced in the art of constructing narrative exposition, but before you, Dear Reader, give up in confusion, let me clarify what I myself finally realized on the second or third reading, and that is that the house, which is the setting of the story at this point, was home to the dog, Danny Lunder, and to the kitten, Jane, but also to another, older (don't ask her age) female cat named Maisie. But, of course, there will be more on Maisie later. Now, back to the letter … E.T.)*

He had found the letters some time on the very morning of the same day that the boy and his mother came, the same day … But that's another part of the story too, much later. Anyway, who knows exactly which date or what time it was; right about then, he had stopped caring about what the time was. Jane hadn't been inside the house in whatever time it is that is too long.

A little pile of papers they were—hers, no doubt about that. As a dog, especially a retrieving one, he could identify and remember even a faint scent all his life—in fact, even a scent that had been around years before his life began. So much for time and all the fuss it brings about. He thought he'd heard that Labradors, regardless of color, have even more remarkable noses, than, say, your average Collie, but he'd never known a Collie. In any case, when he smelled that particular scent, whenever the day was, he knew the papers were Jane's, yes, but didn't know why or exactly what else he would like to know about them. His nose had clogged up with emotion after a few sniffs, and he could hardly receive any extra details. To tell the truth, he was half angry also that he didn't know what they were exactly, that she hadn't told him anything about them. He had thought he was her truest friend, maybe even before the human woman, the Mistress.

And he had come upon them entirely by accident:

During the day, even in these lately strange times, even with her gone, he still traveled the routes he did in the past when he went in search of her, the paths they'd used when she was still a kitten; they had often played a sort of hide and seek action, a planned and unplanned game. She would deliberately hide—behind the half-open bathroom door, for instance—and wait until he came very close; then, she'd leap out toward his head, and he'd pretend he hadn't smelled where she was all along, and he'd give a little surprise yelp. And she'd roll on her back and cup his nose in her two front paws just like she wanted to climb up over his ears to the top of his head, and all the while, she'd be gently scraping at his chest with her back paws; "puntering," she called it. Then, she might use her back legs to crouch and work in a strange sort of back and forth movement, "rantering," she called that, so she could push off and she could chase him this time. There were times he'd find her hiding when she did not want the game, when she would want to be sleeping, and just to let him know this, she'd whip out a paw with its claws exposed and hold it there steady about an inch from his face until he backed away. He had learned from Maisie that cats are unpredictable creatures, especially about sleeping, and although he decided he would not call them lazy exactly, no, still he did begin to think that they also have very self-centered ways, ways of ignoring duty and the wishes of others whenever they liked. He had come to realize that a dog has to learn to accept the cat's ways, in the interest of ... self-preservation as in the case of Maisie, and in the interest of friendship, as in the case of Jane. And, after she was gone, he would sit in the hallway with his nose close to the top railing where she had always rubbed her cheek, and he would become sad to think about the past, all that learning about good friends, then also about the very present, to think he'd be so lonely as to wander about, tracking her old scent, when he knew it was old and he knew she was gone. He could only think he did it out of some kind of human-type hope response, hope of finding her again, safe inside the house, curled up in some usual corner or another. *(Some would call it "denial." E.T.)*

And so it was that he eventually found the letters.

One of the places he used to look for both cats when all else failed was up on a certain shelf in the spare bedroom's closet. The Mistress kept boxes of old clothing, blankets and towels, all sorts of odd materials, on the shelves in that closet, and he checked this area pretty regularly; it was just that, this time, while he was sniffing up toward the second shelf and along under each other box, he discovered, at the corner of one, a scent of Jane's that was stronger than he had remembered, stronger than that of Maisie's or the Mistress; yes, there at the bottom corner of one fairly new blue box was *she*! He may have called out in excitement. He stopped. He sat down, his head to the side. He was certain that, in the past, he had smelled only the Mistress in this box. He stood up and felt his tail jumping with excitement, then slowing down with confusion as he considered how the scent could truly be Jane's. How would he have missed her here so far? Both cats slept any and everywhere they wanted, unlike him, but he couldn't think he'd grown careless enough to overlook the quality of odors in this one of their special places. Well, but then... He sniffed again. No mistake! His tail was swinging again! Someone must have moved the box around, turned it toward the front. Turned it. Moved it. He looked behind himself to see ... what might be ... if there might be a chair to stand on? Probably not. Well, shortly he gave a little jump and braced both front legs on the first shelf; then, standing up on his back legs, holding himself with his front left paw on the shelf, he placed his right paw on the top right corner of the box; he set his right paw on the edge of the corner of the box, and then he saw his paw move as it pulled the box, as the box came over onto his head and chest, and fell—not exactly unexpectedly—to the floor, and he—not exactly accidentally— then found Jane's letters. They lay strewn between some strips of yellow polka-dotted cotton. It *was* she! There was the strong, unmistakable scent again! For just a brief second, the letters were to him the real presence of his kitten, that dusty gray and creamy clouded Jane Seymore. And for a second, he expected his nose to touch her cool nose, to slide along her neck fur, to find his own licking scents mixed with hers at the base of her ear, and at the

same time, for a moment, he heard her low, light whimperings…
before he knew they were his.

The questions still bothered him: Why hadn't his nose detected such papers before? And why had he not even known Jane had written them? A mystery. "A dog doesn't like too much mystery," he thought. But "a bone is a bone," his mother often said, "regardless of its origin." He set to work at once on this one.

He carefully sorted the papers out from between the dotted material and gathered them up, still making those soft wet sounds of whimperings. He took the now damp pile of letters with him to his bed; he knew he'd have a few hours to go over them and decide what to do before the Master came home. He was thinking of hiding them some place right there, under his sleeping pad, for instance. Not the most unusual place for hiding. He was aware of the way humans hid things under their pads; he'd noticed lots of things under the Master's, from magazines to money. If this was typical of many species, then, most anyone looking for something would look under sleeping pads right away. Well. But he wanted to keep the letters close, near him, for a few days at least.

(*As it turned out, Danny tells me, no one looked for anything under his bed pad, not at all; no one even touched the surface of it, much less removed it for a shake or cleaning, as had the Mistress. And certainly no one looked there or anywhere else for a pile of letters from a little stray cat named Jane. Least of all the Master. No, not at all. E.T.*)

And so the letters went under his bed pad, but as fate would have it, Danny had not a moment to read the letters that day or for some days after. That day marked the beginning of a confusing and temporarily disappointing time for Danny, but he is getting ahead of the story. There is plenty of room for telling all of the story in its time, in order.

In the meanwhile, let it just be said, that according to Danny, when he did finally read the letters, he learned more about Jane than he'd known before, and there were things he wished he had known before, but by then it was too late. "Isn't that just the way things can turn out and they turn out that way too much," he thought. "Maybe," he thought, "she didn't think her thoughts were important enough to tell me about at the time, or maybe she didn't trust me the way I thought she did, but if she had told me more, I could have helped her more. Cuhruff." He did not think to say exactly that we make strangers of ourselves all the time, even with those of our own species, but especially when we're with others.

Well! But there it was: the reason to set the letters out for everyone. For all to read.

Yes, and that's why, at some time along the way, he decided to arrange the letters she wrote in a form that everyone could read and understand. And although many may not care about what happens to a rather messy looking, orphaned, and helpless gray kitten, Danny feels that they should care; he thinks, they should care and thereby help reduce the strangeness between us all. And so, because it is fairly commonly understood, English is the language he chose to use.

And (*with help from the translator*), he has written a little introductory note for the letters:

> Dear Reader, I have decided to put forth these letters for the purpose of the edification of all, nonhuman and human animals alike. (*Danny becomes rather formal, even conservative in written expression, when he is explaining about the letters, perhaps in an effort to create a sense of intellectual credibility on his part. E.T.*) Through them, we will come to know and love everyone! To sniff and lick without a growl or curling lip. To live in harmony together so that we will not ruin anyone else's house or yard with our, well, with all our individual droppings. (*He also seems to have become something of a liberal in terms of thought— hopefully, not what one would go so far as to call "New Age"—as a result of his letter experience, and although most of his ideas have been expressed previously and more elegantly by others, and despite his being entirely sincere, when all is said and done, these "feel good" ideas may alienate the very readers he so hopes to reach*

with his messages. But, in the end, we must try to be tolerant of those who feel extra strongly about the principles of good will because so many creatures, as Danny Lunder fears, don't feel anything much about them at all. E.T.)

In this hope I set out the letters of Jane. By way of introduction, I can say that I came to know Jane in the fall of the "Two Hurricanes" year, which was then last year, and that we lived at that time as brother and sister along with a second cat named Maisie in a two-story house belonging to a man and woman who ... Well, I can see E.T. shaking her head, so I think we will stop and let the letters themselves tell what they have to say themselves.

Finally, I want to thank Jane and the many others who gave of ...

(The reader may note that the names of the "many others" to be thanked are missing from the final sentence above. Yes. And now, in order not to blame anyone by name, along with the politicians, I will use the passive voice and say: "a mistake was made." Here we see that "someone" must have forgotten to fill in the names of all the people and animals, including his mother, who helped the dog in the telling of the story. Perhaps the editor should have caught this error. Perhaps she did, but ... chose not to point it out, chose to go on without it. Perhaps she thought she could attach a list the helpers in an appendix, later, if necessary, together with anything else that had been "forgotten." Thanks for your patience. E.T.)

P.S. Now, let be said that this whole project will be a surprise for Jane. We know how she had hidden the letters away, so we think she must have felt reluctant to expose them to the world in the form in which they were written. Imagine her pleasure to see them so neatly done up and easy to read as they will be when they are set out here before us!

Now I say, with good will to all, ON WITH THE LETTERS! D.L.

JANE LETTER #1

Dear Mahrowh,

There is no expectation in me that you will ever read this letter—or even that you will ever receive it—for I don't know that I will ever be able to send it to you properly, but I miss being next to you so much that I think my loneliness can be relieved if I make believe I am speaking to you, telling you what is happening to me and how I am doing. For I know very well that you are wondering and may be worrying about me in your loving way. I even thought, with a wild jump away from reason, that if I wrote down my words, they would make their way to your heart, even though your eyes might never see them. And, in return, my heart would be eased as well. If only I could feel one of your firm, rough licks on my ear right now, I would half close my eyes and tilt up my chin and make a roaring purr, loud as a foot massager, back up to your ear.

The dog here does a job of licking me sometimes, but as you know, a dog's tongue is far too smooth for a decent cleansing, although it's plenty firm enough to knock one over! Speaking of a decent cleansing, I don't want even to begin to describe what has been called the "doggy odor" or how prominently it clings to this dog's tongue, and especially, I resist a confession that I have grown to like it.

> *(Dear Reader, Danny Lunder wants me to interrupt here to say that he will try not to interrupt the letters but he does want to say that he does not object when Jane criticizes him, even for things he can't help, like his tongue being smooth, and he also wants me to say that he did learn not to knock her over as she got bigger. He would like also to point out some other things, but, as his editor, I have convinced him (again) that*

such a digression is distracting to whatever plot he may want to develop and that he must stop and let the letters go on. Which he has done. E.T.)

Anyhow, I don't need someone to clean me; I'm surely able to keep myself presentable by myself, as you showed me, but I like this dog to lick me anyway because, well, of course, because it reminds me of you and all of us tumbling around together, so warm and safe in that closet by the food room. But now, I'm getting too far ahead in what happened.

First, you'll want to know about Boots and me on that parting day, the day we disappeared from you. Now, I don't want to upset you; you know there was nothing you could have done to keep any of this from happening. You know, as I well know now, that we have very little we can do to set our lives in a direction we might ourselves determine, and perhaps we wouldn't know where our own direction would lead either, even if we could determine it. I wonder. But you were shut in the food room when the man picked me up along with my sister and carried us to the other door. I have to tell you we did not struggle or try to wiggle away. We had not ever known this human to cause pain. And so we were confused to see that the little girl with my name, Jane, had water dripping from her eyes and so did the woman beside her, if one can judge by the sniffing sounds she made, and Jane's voice made sounds like those we heard when she fell down the stairs that one day and spilled the ice cream or when she didn't want to go up the stairs to sleep at night.

By the way, I am learning lots more Human words since I left you, but I still remember ours. I say them sometimes to remind me of earlier times, but I need to practice using Human so I can become more aware of what might happen to me or of what *is* happening to me! Not to be taken by surprise is a good thing, usually. Although I think some surprises work out well. Remember the time we saw three pop bugs come out from under the potato bin, one for each of us!

(I, as your editor, will try to tolerate Jane's ignorance of just about everything, especially of certain well-known living species, particularly my own, such as when she refers to insects as "bugs." E.T.)

It's just that I regret not having tried to escape that day. Had I known what it meant when the man carried us across the room to that other door, what it meant to be carried *out* of that door, I would never, never have gone easily; I would have twisted and scratched and howled and bitten; I would have squeezed free and slid bumping down to the floor, and from there, leapt like a tree frog high onto a shelf or vanished like smoke into a low and dark place; under a bed is very good, usually, for us. But not a box, no...

Oh! I forgot! There were boxes everywhere! Do you remember? What racing and hiding we did around and between and inside those boxes! And remember! One was almost full of some kinds of materials ... I didn't know the name for them then; were they what are called "towels"? And we all fell asleep on and under those soft pieces of cloth just as the clock struck three in the morning. And the humans laughed when they found us there at breakfast.

Now, I see these memories brighter than I could have imagined them to be, slipping into my eyes before I can blink. Maybe the water that comes from the eyes will soon rinse everything regretful away. I will stop now and wait for that rinsing to happen, as I remain,
Your kitten,
Jane

JANE LETTER #2

Dear Mahrowh again,

I'm going ahead with all this writing in spite of my memories and sadness because I am told it will be helpful for me to reconstruct my early days; this advice comes from the dog who lives here. As is most likely for a dog, I think he must have picked it up from a human in that usual canine effort to be all things to all people. I just can't imagine a cat wallowing around sorting out memories of unpleasant deeds or events from the past. "Yurough!" The dog tells me that the harder it is to look the pain, the more one must need to do it. Well, that sounds like some kind of punishment to me, and punishment doesn't seem fair. In the end, however, when the looking has been done, according to this dog, I am going to feel free as a bird (his peculiar analogy) and light as a feather (same idea). Or maybe it was the other way around.

In any case, it's true that when I think of you and how bewildered you must have been to discover us gone, Boots and me, I can only hope that you took one last look at those old memories and stored them safely away. I hope that your mind has come to think mostly of the place where you are now, which place I wish I knew, perhaps still in the one where we all were together in the beginning, with the human Jane and that group, or maybe with a new family, even new babies, and new memory-making days.

Although we don't linger on it, explore it, excuse or justify it, we cats will accept the memory of a hurtful thing, I believe, but my hope is for you to be happy now. Speaking of now, you may notice I call myself a cat now even though I don't know if I truly am one yet. What *does* make the difference? Because of all I have endured, I somehow feel older than I must be. Is that a usual feeling? But if age is a state of mind, I may be older than I am! "Rowowha!"

(These two or three paragraphs represent the first of many containing philosophical conjectures bordering on ideas found in the ubiquitous self-help books of my generation; I could suggest that the reader skip over them, but unfortunately, it is not always possible to divorce them from the narrative with its necessary exposition. E.T.)

Well, old or young, cat or kitten, the same thing happened: when the man went out of the door carrying Boots and me, we both hid our heads in the crook of his arm and tried to crawl in after them. Then, he had a box that he put us in and covered with a cloth, and he carried us, walking, walking, and walking … a long way it seemed, until he stopped and took Boots out. The moment Boots began her crying and I couldn't see her, that was the moment I felt a little prickle of fear along my back and into my tail. My fur went up then for the very first time, and I remember feeling that strange tight pull and slight wavering; I heard myself cry out too; I felt myself twist upright also, along with my hairs, then stand on back feet and scratch high into a corner to be out of that box and beside Boots wherever she was. But the man turned quickly and moved away quickly, farther and farther away. I could hear Boots' cries and mine together until there were only mine left, alone. Well, my body went into action at that point, almost beyond any control, my claws ripping into the corners of that box at a dreadful rate. When the man's hand came in slowly under the cloth to push me back down, I'm afraid it got ripped up along with the box, and he removed it at once; he removed it with words of anger that must not be repeated by a well-raised animal. (At least I figure that is so; to tell the truth, the only times I'd heard this man speak, he'd used words that the woman said shouldn't be used in front of their child, and he wasn't even suffering from needle-pointed kitten claws then. Of course, he hadn't been around much during our time at that house. Maybe I'm not being fair to assume he always spoke that way. Maybe he was suffering a lot when he was around the woman and child. "Eur.") Anyway, I could tell he was angry, but that did not prevent him from walking away, away and away.

When this person finally put the box down and pulled off the covering, at first I saw only space, a large, open area, then, a porch, some kind of mat in front of a small bowl ... I can't say of what, and a newspaper. (I learned some of these words later, like "bushes.") Bushes grew on both sides of the porch and steps and, without waiting longer that it takes to say, "dog off leash'", I bolted from the box and the porch right into the largest bush I saw. I guess I thought anywhere else was better than being in that box, going farther and farther away from Boots, not to mention you. Or maybe at times like that, one doesn't think at all in the regular sense of the word.

(Jane obviously obeyed the primitive fight/flight reaction people speak of; I hesitate to say "instinct" because that concept is just such a controversial one these days. E.T.)

The branches stuck in and out of my legs, but I finally ended up on the ground. Where I stayed. I stayed so still you wouldn't have believed me to be a kitten at all. I was like one of those stuffed cats people put on chairs and other people think are real.

And it wasn't long before I realized the man was gone. "But," I thought, "he may not have gone far enough."

So, as it grew dark under the bushes and, then, even darker, I stayed in that place.

Later, I don't know how much later, I heard footsteps and voices on the porch; after some more time, lights came on both inside and out. I heard voices and singing behind the porch door.

I stayed under the bushes. The nights were not cold then, so I wondered at the way I was shaking, and at the tiny "murouwh" sounds I heard myself making as if I had no control over my expressions at all.

Gradually, the sounds in the house died away and, soon, each inside light dropped off too. There was only a splash left on the porch from a bulb outside and above me.

For a long while, I remembered the bowl on the porch. Yes, I kept it in my mind for a long time. I decided it probably had cat food in it. Surely, I would have heard the sounds of a dog eating supper by now if there were a dog around. I have since come to have affection for the dog I know here, but still, I have to say; there is nothing quiet about a dog at a food bowl.

As my mind wandered around that bowl of food and imagined what it would be like to eat every pellet down to the bottom, I heard what was for me then a very unusual swashing and shuffling sound on the sidewalk; this was followed by a scraping and clicking sound on the porch steps. For the second time in less than 24 hours, my back and tail fur rose up, and my mind left the food behind to listen, to listen for any additional, maybe recognizable, sound nearby. Nothing but more swash and click, until l heard... "Eurah!" Crunching! There it was: a definite crunching. Well, I could recognize that sound all right. And it was the sound, of course, of my food being eaten up by whatever it was that had swashed and clicked its way to that bowl and was now crunching away there at a very measured pace, at an even, relaxed sounding pace. There it was.

After a while, the food was gone. I could tell that, of course, because the crunching stopped, and the swashing and clicking began again, across the porch and down the steps, into the grass, growing softer and softer, and then, along with the cat food, gone.

And the night exploded after that time into a kind of lively darkness for me. I began to hear crackling and scuffling and soft whispering sounds close to my sides, there, there, and here, then above me, in the porch boards, everywhere; I could hear human voices laughing from a distance away and an off-and-on whirring of what I later learned to be the motors and tires of moving cars.

After a while, I wondered if perhaps there might be a morsel or two left in the porch bowl. And much later, as some early light appeared, I crept from under the bushes, climbed the steps, reached the porch, and found the bowl to be empty, quite empty, after all. I didn't even bother to lick the bottom.

Back into the bushes I went, and I crouched again to wait. To wait for what? I didn't have any idea at first. But it's strange the way the mind can grow so full of thinking about nothing. This is the condition that happened to me there in that new situation, one I'd never been in before. Images of possibilities appeared in my head and dreams, but strange images: a food bowl large as a porch, spills over, kibbles the size of light bulbs; a black storm in a racing wind sweeps everything up into a whirlpool, food and porch boards swirling in a funnel and down a huge bathtub drain; everything knocking against everything else and when the giant soap suds appear, they cover the whole area. You have to close your eyes to keep them from stinging. And when you open them, not one bite-sized, dry and crispy kibble is left. Well, my life was about to become full of these unknown kinds of situations, more than one a day, and I'd say looking back and forward, more to come for many more days to come. Churning about in various ways.

Were you ever in such circumstances, I wonder?

And so ended the first night I spent on my own, my first night of freedom, you could say if you wanted to look at it that way, or of fear, you would say if you wanted to look at it the way I did that night.

I look now and I see you, Mahrowh, sleeping warm and still behind my eyes; I see the bowl beside you, and in it is a good portion of dry kibble, the size of kitten paw pads, lying very still. I see both you and the bowl, exactly where you should be, waiting, and deep in my heart, comfort.

Your kitten,
Jane

JANE LETTER #3

Dear Mahrowh,

I must admit that, for all of the first night, so alone and fearful, and for all of the next day, I remained under those bushes; then, by the next night, the empty spaces in my stomach began pulling in tight and causing a bunch of jostling pains to shoot out into various parts of my body.

There had been many noises and much movement all day long around the porch. Some sounds I could distinguish a bit, young and old voices, for instance, and one I couldn't help but unhappily realize to be the churrup of a cat. I waited. I waited, but by now I was not waiting with the full patience of a grown cat. I waited like a kitten.

Out of the corner of my eye I kept seeing twitches in the old leaves and other dying material that piled itself up against the side of the porch and around the trunk of my hiding bush. I tried, nevertheless, to be properly still. I waited until I was bursting with energy, literally trembling with pent up leaping power, my hind legs paletta runting under my haunches, revved up to spring me forward onto whatever was causing a disturbance in the area.

Sometimes, when I'd leap, I'd find it was all a hoax; I'd find nothing under a particular leaf to grab onto, so I'd have to pretend. I'd pretend that everywhere I looked the leaves were full of beetles or those large black water bugs we used to find in the pantry. *(Oh, indeed! Those nasty things in the pantry. One would never find their like in the library. Of course not!! E.T.)* I remember how you moved those fat beetles from side to side with a gentle paw or touched their hard backs, pushing down just a little, like a tickle, to help them wiggle; you showed us how to encourage everybody to play. So, I hope you won't be disappointed when I tell you that what I did that

17

day did not resemble your typical predator play-practice session much less the carefully organized precision action of a well-oiled killing machine. As they say. What I did after my first jump was that I kept on jumping; I jumped forward, backward, and sideways; I jumped up and turned around in the air. I threw dry leaves to the sky and rooted under and up the wet, resting ones; I tore holes in some that were too heavy to move. I pounced here and there as if beetles and water bugs covered every inch of the ground, as if the leaves were teeming with insects of super powers who taunted me and needed no encouragement to play, and, as the action increased, I was rolling, thrashing and lashing out, in every direction. I defeated creatures of monstrous proportions, beside every leaf, one by one. I forgot your advice to take things easy and prolong the fun. In the end, I lay exhausted in the middle of my battlefield and took a nap. When I woke up, I couldn't find a single carcass. Imagination can be an invaluable resource during times of boredom, but, also can lead to an embarrassment, like the time I jumped on Boots in the litter box. And a rush into fantasy takes a lot of energy.

One can't last long in battle when carrying around an empty stomach.

Now, you might wonder why, if I were so hungry, I didn't plan things out and work in a more organized manner to catch something around there to eat. And I can only answer: I don't know. I don't know why it never occurred to me, at that time, even to taste a bit of any bug that I later grew pretty good at destroying. After we finished playing with them in the pantry, why didn't you and I and Boots eat those fat water bugs with the hard wing coverings? I can only think that you must know something, Mahrowh, something we did not know about such meals.

After resting a while, I worked at keeping my tail still.

As the world's light grew dim that second day and the porch lights came on, I could smell food and hear sounds of voices inside again. I crept out from under the bush to the bottom of the steps; I crept half way up on the edge and crouched and waited in that kind of half-way nap we cats use to save energy. After a long time in my minutes, the woman came out, picked up the empty bowl, and put a full one down in its place. As she turned to go back inside, she called, "Kitty, Kitty, Kitty. Come along, Kitty, Kitty." "Well," I thought, "How good it is of her to call me like that!" She practically sang out those words, "Kitty, Kitty," just like our other woman had. Wouldn't it mean the same? Then, she was gone and the door was closed, and I was beside the bowl before I heard the lock turn. I took one whiff, a small sniff, just to be polite, then I began gobbling up food in the way cats usually don't. That is, I did not lick or chew tentatively as if I were bored with the same old thing. In fact, I didn't chew at all except every third or fourth pellet ... or fifth.

And I didn't see or smell the black inkblot of a mass before it landed on the far side of the porch, and I only vaguely heard its timer, a low almost inaudible growl, as it slow-motioned its way toward me. Then, it stopped. Finally, I turned to look, and with a yowl, the black mass landed right in front of me, becoming a massive furry object that I knew to be an angry cat. Of course, it was. "Rowowah". Its size could have been partly a result of the battle hairs that rose up all over the head, body and tail. I didn't take a close look at the fur. I was committed to my ears, and they told me to leave quickly; they assured me this was not a standoff situation for me. I hesitated only a moment before I began placing one paw behind the other, backing, backing away until I fell off the edge of the porch. Unable to right myself fast enough, in a second, the fur and weight closed over me, clinging on all sides, rolling me around as if I were now a water beetle in the leaves. I opened my claws and mouth; I chopped and grabbed here and there but touched nothing, held only open space between claws and teeth. Then, as it turned to be on top, I pushed my back legs hard against its belly, and being small enough, I slipped out from between the black legs, and shook myself free. I assume the furry mass was hungry enough to leave me and go back to the food bowl at about the same time I left him to go anywhere else!

He may not have eaten all the food in that bowl, but I would not wait there to eat it. I gathered four legs under my own belly and sprang forth into the darkness like a rabbit. For lack of knowing better, I was probably looking to find something else to go under, a bush or maybe a dry porch with padded bushes around it. But, as I ran, I thought this: Although it's true that one might be safe living under a porch, in the long run, hummf, how rich and varied a life would one have … under a porch? As you always said in the boxes, Mahrowh, we won't be playing with tissue paper and towels all our lives. That's right. And all in all, even with the dangers, and despite the fun and games in the leaves, the prospects of building a productive future while located entirely under a porch looked pretty bleak. "Urough."

So, I ran. I don't know for how long or in what direction. And when I stopped, all worn out, I crawled into a space under a large, dark object; it stretched out about 13 times larger than a standard litter box. It had no bushes near it, but I was so tired by then that I disregarded that observation and thought only a moment of where Boots might be, in what direction, before I fell asleep.

And so my second night began.

(There is a break at this point in this letter, and when it continues, it continues on a different kind of paper. Where all this writing material is coming from, at this point, I do not know. E.T.)

Along about midnight I think it was, I heard a familiar swash and clicking sound and awakened to an apparition: a white ghost-like nozzle moving slowly along beside my space and face. I hissed loudly—with no reaction; the thing kept right on swashing and clicking; slowly it went, but it did keep moving. I waited (Waiting has become something I do better and better.) and watched, then finally made a turn around and tried to sleep again. Without much success. The ground below me was rough with loose rocks.

At some time close after the first light, I was stretching out when I saw a human coming towards my place. I slipped back underneath whatever it was I had been under before just as the human disappeared above me, disappeared right into my very cover! With a bang! "Oh, rowghwa!" I could think of nothing normal, and then, of a sudden, a spit of motor-like noise sprayed out above me, splashing and sinking over all sides. Then extra strange noises. Loud ones. I froze. And of course, all my back and tail hairs stood up at attention again, something I was getting tired and more tired of feeling.

"Oughow!" It moved! The object over me was moving! The noises continued, and the object moved—or, for a moment, I thought maybe the space under me moved. I was terrified and stiff with fear until, all at once, part of the thing was coming toward me and I was jolted into action, out from under that one into the midst of countless others, some moving and some still. No trees, no bushes, nothing I recognized. I turned in a circle. The original object turned with me, and I stepped back, and another appeared beside me; I turned away, and another slid behind. Tubes of smoke wrapped themselves around my eyes; sprays of motor noises, dripping their harsh greasy odors, swiped at my ears and nose, louder and louder, until, finally, I leapt up and away. To the left, to the right. I ran. I headed nowhere I could name, but anywhere there was space.

(When Jane told Danny parts of this story after they met, he explained that cars are more fun to be in than under. I wouldn't know or care to know myself. E.T.)

Finally, I felt the soft green under my feet and, off to the sides, I could see long walkways and bushes with houses in the centers of them. What a relief! Of course, we know now that a house is no guarantee of safety, don't we? But bushes ... Well, and where there was a house, there might be a porch to go under and ... I know, I know; I only considered moving backwards: Bushes and porches ... did I really think they would lead me to a better future? Maybe not. But for now, I was thinking, "I just want to feel safe. I just want to turn toward something familiar and worry about the future later. Doesn't one have to rely on what makes one feel safe? In times of turmoil? At least at first?" That's what I was thinking.

So, I approached a bush, about three-boxes high and shiny-leafed. But even as I lowered my belly and put one paw in front of the other, I was struck with a new thought: "Under a bush" might not be any safer than outside of one. For the love of turkey necks, a bush could have any number of fearful possibilities lying under it. What about ... pincher bugs? *(Here we go again. E.T.)* or what about just about anything one couldn't see in advance? My dear Mahrowh, I was discovering the whole impossibility of knowing what is safe and what is not. I had thought I knew what "Kitty, Kitty" was, hadn't I? And with the call of "Kitty, Kitty," food did appear, but did not also appear the angry cat that leapt out right behind the food. That and all the bushes and all the porches have now made me feel very unclear about safety anywhere.

So, despite all these various thinkings, I went under a bush again. And as I scratched around to be comfortable among the cold and wet and old and dried up leaves (some with hard, dried-up points on them) I had another thought, which is that, sometimes, one has no opportunity to debate the meanings or the safety of her actions; sometimes, the only thing left to do is to do something, and if going under the first available bush is what there is to do, so be it. I went under, and I crouched and waited again. As my heart returned to its normal speed, I waited. I fell into a little cat nap and heard, in patchwork dreams, my breath go in and out with little sighs. Truly, I was ready to stop, to stop all activity.

To rest a while.

I stayed under that particular bush for some long length of cat time, coming out for water I found in a nearby bowl. Well, this was a very large and also multipurpose bowl, and besides drinking it, some birds splashed the water all over their bodies, which is why they called the place a bird bath. I jumped in there among the birds on that first day and jumped back out when they rose to the sky with noisy power and water blops dropping from their wings.

I ate a few sluggish bugs from time to time as the days grew cooler, but my own energy was slugging down too, taking to ground along with the brown leaves and grasshoppers. After a while, I had no desire to hunt at all, even something as catchable as a 12-hour moth. I grew more and more tired and wanted nothing else but to stay curled up as safe as I knew it to be under my own quiet bush.

And would have done that, I think, had it not been for Jake.

(Dear Reader, this is an interruption by Danny and me for the purpose of saying that we think this particular letter becomes a little long. I write as "we," but then, no, the truth comes out that, when he first read this letter, Danny became so emotionally wrought up that he felt the need of a short break himself or, he tells me, he felt his heart would break. I do not have anything of what one would be likely to call a heart, so I had no idea what he was talking about. Then, he tells me that humans have hearts also, and it occurred to him that you, Dear Reader, as human, might appreciate a relief from the emotional demands being put upon you here. As an aside, Danny tells of some encounters he had with the black cat mentioned above, meetings he recalls from his walks as a puppy and so on, and that the above mentioned cat appeared to be somewhat aggressive when it came to food but not a bad fellow overall. Jane must have caught him at the wrong moment, according to Danny Lunder. Having no experience with a heart or that particular cat, I will not comment for the moment, except to warn the reader to take a deep breath and expect even more situations resulting from and in misunderstandings and misjudgments of both hearts and cats. Now, to continue:)

Had it not been for Jake, I wouldn't have found enough food to survive, nor would I have found the house with Danny in it. But again, I'm going ahead too fast. Here is how it happened:

Picture a night after the days have grown shorter for me and are becoming dark very early. This is the first night I remember finding myself too tired to move even at the sound of a strange nearby light flickering off and on; I've been lying flat, almost motionless, now for some time among the old damp leaves. But this night I do hear faintly, somewhere in my head, a sound I know from other nights; it's that same swash and clicking I've heard on porches and driveways since I was first thrown away. This time, I don't have any will to move at all, but even without much strength, I can turn my head and see for sure who belongs to those sounds: I see a mouse-colored figure, in the shape of an egg, a longish egg; at one end it shows a thin tail, grey and without the comfort of any fur around it; at the other end the egg shape narrows into a triangular white face that goes on into a quite sharply pointed nose-like mouth and a set of sharply pointed teeth which hold…which hold in them a large and chunky chicken leg bone; I can smell it fresh. Everything stops. And, and then, right then and there, I watch the two paws move up, and I see the longest paw nails I have ever seen surround and reposition the chicken bone between the teeth… And it's all so close to me that I dare not move, even breathe. But I can smell the fresh meat, so when the pointy-nose mouth settles the bone securely, and its body slowly swashes and clicks its way down the walk, I get my legs up and follow after, also slowly. I see the creature stop at a wooden fence, and there I see him drop the chicken bone. He climbs up the fence and knocks off something that sounds like metal, and then I can hear him snorting around inside of what must be a trash or garbage container. Though I can't see the top of the container itself, pretty soon I can see all kinds of papers, cans, clear and colored wrappings, all sorts of things, floating or tumbling onto the ground and lying just inside and under the fence. Well, soon then, after all that trouble, finally there are chunks and splats of actual meat and other editable foods flopping onto the confused ground, too. As for me, I wait, as usual, in my naturally cautious way but due also to my unusual lack of energy at this point. I wait, but not long; soon the sight and scent of that first dropped bone takes over and I jump, grab and retreat all in one swift movement. I hide in shadows and watch whatever falls, as I chew the fat, juicy chunks left on that miracle leg.

You can imagine, Mahrowh, just how lucky I felt in those moments.

(*Lucky or not, you may have noticed, as I did, Dear Reader, how immediately Jane has assumed the masculine pronoun for this creature even though she had no information as to the sex of the animal at that time. This assumption could be the result of laziness or ignorance or it could be an indication of cultural sexism. My bet is that it involves all three, but predominately the latter. When I spoke to Danny about it, he, being male himself, did not seem to care about any difference it would make. E.T.)*

So began our nightly rounds. I followed as Mr. Sniffer wobbled for hours from drive way to porch to trash basket to garbage can. For all its pointedness, that nose of his had an amazing ability to sniff out edibles. Well, usually the stuff was edible, for him at least, and after he finished, I could usually bring myself to swallow a mouthful or two, even if I could seldom identify what it was I was swallowing. At several places, there might be a dish containing the remnants of a meal of real cat food that some poor disappointed feline was going to miss after I ate it. At each stop, as the night went on, there was more food left over for me, even though, because of its strangeness, I could not yet eat all of it. Maybe I was not hungry enough, but I believe it just isn't in my nature to eat garbage easily, even the best of it, unless nothing else is available.

So, this routine was our nightly routine. I kept well behind my sniffing buddy, let him finish up and move on before I'd take a bite. He never saw me. At first, I thought his eyes were bad. He paid no attention to me as I waited in the shadows. He'd eat and move on. Then, I'd eat and move on. I never had trouble catching up with him later; this creature moved so slowly and made so much noise that I kept being surprised he didn't get into more trouble than he did. Sometimes, a human would shout from a door or window at him and he'd swash along a little faster than usual.

During the day, I didn't want to lose sight of my restaurant guide for fear he might set forth on our twilight cafeteria meal trail without me. You know Mah how you used to tell us not to let something good out of sight, that a bird under the paw is worth two in the air. Well, each morning, when we'd finished eating, I could see my chef go into a hole he had dug under a small backyard shed, and so one day I became very brave and climbed into the upper part through a broken window. I should admit, too, that the water drops were falling that morning pretty thick. (Since then, in a continuing effort to improve my language skills, I am calling these drops "rain.") Anyway, once inside the shed, I see it is a place where there are tools like rakes and shovels and also odors very much like those unpleasant and unhealthy and unnatural ones in our pantry room at home, but I notice some additional scents, too, nice ones of damp wood and earth and the dried hard tops of dead beetles. So, after looking the place over, I select a yellow, open-slatted crate to sleep in. I go on to scratch up some of the newspapers piled at one end and make a little nest. This bed reminds me only a little of you and Boots and of the boxes where we lived. During the day, I can hear my pointy-nosed food-finder turning around in his under-the-shed bed whenever a dream or a siren wakes him briefly, and I do feel some little, soft comforting moments at times in our shed, dozing and waking, with the rain on the tin roof and knowing there will be something to eat later.

And now I will tell you how I finally came to meet in person the animal that led me to the food that saved me, the one who saved your own kitten's life.

So, it had been raining, as I say, but as we do expect, after a while, a day and night in this case, the rain will begin to drip slower and slower, and pretty soon I do hear my traveling chef clamber out of his shed hole and begin slupping around in the muddy grass that had once been the solid yard; the mud that has taken over the yard has also taken some of the swash out of his walk, but he manages to push enough grass down to make a sort of trench path. I follow as he makes his way slowly out toward the house behind the shed. Then, kabunckock, both of us stop sharply at the sight of a full-to-bulging paper bag of fresh garbage sitting right in front of us, waiting right there in front of us, in the middle of our yard. "Someone had not wanted to get wet going to the can", I think. "Or maybe the can was full." Well, in any case and in one moment and at the same time that Mr. Pointy-Nose pushes like a bull dozer into that slippery, wet bag, I loose all control. Before I can think "flea meds," I leap forward and with the sound of a smoke alarm land right smack on top of my special meal buddy. Both of us hold still a moment as we sink slowly and slowly down right through the middle of the very mushy dinner rolls and corn flakes that are by now squeezing themselves out of their containers. "Oughow!"

"Woooup," says a voice I can only call raspy. In a jolt, Mr. Pointy Nose steps back away from the garbage, and I slide down with a swash. When he speaks in our language of Cat, his pointy nose works in connection with his mouth and both move in a shuffling way as do his legs: "Hey there, Scruffer," says he, "Now, look at you! For a tiny little whipper you act mighty hungry, so you do. Uh-huh. Well, all right! Just look at this mess! . Boy oh boy, there's here plenty to share. Ummm, um. Feel free to pick your pleasure, have a bite; help yourself; go on and eat up your fill." He smiles sharply. "You're looking at your friendly neighborhood neighbor, so you are, and that's me, so they say."

I, having behaved like such a fool, am at a loss about what to say or do, and sometimes when you're confused for having done one wrong thing, you end up saying or doing another wrong thing, which is what happens to me right then: "But *what* are you?" I say, and there it is. I've just gone and blurted it straight out.

"Well," he says, without seeming at all offended, "there's a lady lives in that old red apartment building calls me a 'damned nuisance', and she does it real loud, so she does." He laughs, and his nose spreads out until he looks almost pleasant.

"Then, there's this other fellow works at the gas station calls me a, well, something in the nature of a 'dirty ole wood rat, enlarged and ugly'." He laughs some more. "But my mother called me a fine specimen of 'opossum', so she did, and I tend to take her word for it as she never led me astray in any other way." He pauses. "You can call me Jake."

"I see." I say. "But then no matter what you are, or who, I can surely say I am sorry I acted so wildly, and I'm glad to meet you at last." I glance at his mouth, as politely as possible, my mouth already opening for one of those bites he's invited me to. So it is that we both begin to eat, face to face, and quickly, for you never know who might show up to spoil your meal. Even so, I can tell, we are feeling the comradeship that comes from breaking bread—or something we hope is edible—together.

Finally, I've had plenty of whatever it is I've eaten (It had tasted a little like fish-flavored cheese spread.), and I sit back to relax a minute before I have to get my fur in order. "My name is- "The words stop coming. I try to cough them up the throat and out, but they sound so sad. I start the cleaning job on my neck and shoulders. Jake is still eating and he doesn't seem to notice any silence. After a little while, I can swallow and say: "My name was, and maybe it still is, Jane. I'm a cat."

"Well, wouldn't I know you're a cat; I know that. I've seen a lot of cats, talked to some, as you can hear, eaten with a few. But you're a small cat, a baby one I'd say. Is that right?"

"I am a baby. I may be about 8 weeks old human time, I think, and it's true I haven't gotten used to being out here alone without a home or … or … Well, you see, he put Boots down in one place and … and he … he put me down … somewhere else … you see, and I … I didn't … I didn't … know … where…" At that point, I begin to feel such a big sadness at the top of my throat again that I just hunch over and I can't speak.

"That's all right. It'll come to you what to say after a while." And after a while, he stops chewing and looks at me more closely. "A bit strange in your coat markings, I'd say, compared to some I've seen."

Well, the truth is, at that time, I'd only ever seen myself briefly, in a puddle of water outside our shed, and I thought I was quite attractive then; a wind was moving the top of the water and I looked all bright and lively. Maybe I only saw for myself. But my dear Mahrowh, you always said I was such a beautiful baby. I remember your words sandwiched between your efficient body licks: "You," you said, stroke, stroke, "are a beautiful," stroke, stroke, "baby kitten," stroke, stroke. But then I remember falling off to sleep as you began to lick Boots, too, and I could hear you saying the same thing to her. "My mother called me beautiful the same as yours did," I reply.

"Um. Well." says Jake. He looks perplexed. And he looks me over some more. "I do like your soft gray background color, so I do, but then you have those messy splashes of orange on top of it, and they fall all over you, no kind of order to be seen. Uh-huh. Not meant to be offensive, you know."

I stand up and look in a current puddle on the sidewalk near our meal; so, I saw: It was true what he was saying. My decorative spots don't seem to be arranged in any sort of classical design, but then, they're not really orange either; they're really a nice, light creamy color, I'd say, fluffy on the edges. They could be clouds. It's true. And Mah, I like them, floating all over as they are. But even if I didn't like them, there they are. And beauty is only skin deep, as we hear said; I don't intend to let my skin—or maybe, in my case, fur also … Well, I'm not sure which the saying refers to, but, in any case, whatever it's called, the colors of it are not going to bother my life.

I turn away from Jake in disappointment. He must just have different color preferences, I reason, and, after all, he's not even a cat. Still, you know how discouraging it is when someone you've just met doesn't seem to like you in some way, especially in one of your main outer aspects.

"Don't worry," Jake goes on to say. "You'll get used to yourself. When I was a little, rat-like thing, I sure didn't like my long hairless tail either, very hard and cold to touch, uh-huh, but as it turns out, an empty tail can be great for sliding through mud; it's got nothing weighty to drag it down and pull it back, and it's so slick nothing can hold onto it for very long, no, it can't. I mean nothing except, I'm told, my very own babies. Don't ask me what it'd be like to have babies on your tail because I can't tell you. Yet. Maybe some day." He turns to contemplate his tail.

In the pause, I turn my head to the side. (I want to be polite.) I don't want to stare, but my eyes slip back to his tail. I view his tail. Well, it may be hairless, hard and cold, but it still has mud all over it just like mine.

Then, Jake laughs and shakes his hips to whip that tail closer. I hope he doesn't want me to touch it; I decide to busy myself with cleaning my own tail.

"So, there it is. He sounds philosophical. "Looks like everything's just … well, just all the way it is." He turns and moves back toward our meal.

29

I watch. Jake's front hands with their long, seemingly awkward nails are very busy setting out scraps of debris (I can not call it food any longer.) in a semicircle in front of him. Once everything is spread out and separated, his nose finds and his sharp little teeth carefully lift out a bite here and there to eat, just the few choice morsels. So, one main benefit of that long pointy face is pretty evident: It can go into any crazy jumble of mixtures and select out to eat specific items of interest without having to taste anything, well, anything distasteful.

Then, I remembered how uncomfortable I'd been in the presence of that face, those scrappy nails, and that tail when I first saw and heard them that one morning. I guess we all have our early judgments.

Oh, my dear Mahrowh, when I think of how little I knew about the world back then, when I was first tossed out. Yes, I'm going to say it as it was: tossed out. Just like that garbage bag itself. As they say, I had no survival skills. Were you ever without a home, I wonder? Or did you always live with the little girl who has my name also. I am sad to think that I know hardly any details of your history or your thoughts, dear Mah. I was so busy being loved and taken care of by you that I paid very small attention to what I might want to know and love about you later.

I end this letter with a wish for better attention to the present in the future. And with a name I will always keep.

Your kitten,

Jane

(*Dear Reader, Danny wants me to mention here that he also wishes he had paid more attention to the details of events during the time that the kitten Jane was with him, there in the house where they met. He says he is thinking that he might have learned more about what was happening to the humans and the animals there; he thinks he might even have prevented some of the disaster that occurred, although I suspect not. I suspect what happened there would have happened anyway. Like a lot of dogs, Danny Lunder will keep on thinking he has much more influence over the way things go than he has; he will never abandon the idea that if he looks up with those big brown eyes and wags his tail, any human within sight of him will put the whole rump of an oven-roasted beef right down on the floor in front of him. I'm here to say: not always so, Danny Lunder, not always so. E.T.*)

JANE LETTER #4

My Dear Mah,

When I ended my last letter, the circumstances of my street life had altered for the better because of finding Jake, and although he admitted he'd never had a kitten stay around with him quite so close for quite so long, he said he didn't mind at all because I did not require much to eat. Of course, the truth is that whereas Jake would eat almost anything (under pressure) when there was a choice, we both preferred protein, especially meat, and I wanted to eat meat that I could smell was safe. So, I think he was mainly being kind when he said he didn't mind my presence; the exact truth is that he has as wide a good-natured generosity about him as his smile.

Jake swished into my life in about ... well, looking back, I think it was early September by then, but as I mentioned before, it was a rainy fall, and one morning in mid-September, we had only just fallen asleep when a fast and whipping wind surprised our day shed, circling and assaulting all parts. At first I kept my eyes closed with the thought that it would soon go away. But the sound of that rushing sweep and whistle seemed to grow louder and louder, until I opened my eyes just half way and saw that wind churn, saw it crash and open up weak old wall boards like tuna cans. Well, then, on top of all that fury, it began to throw down full, fat water drops—I mean to say, "rain"—sideways. By the middle of the first night I was sitting uneasily near the table, just inside the shed door and watching as sticks and leaves floated up higher and higher, bumping along the door sill. About that time, I heard Jake crawling around underneath me and pretty soon, I watched as he bubbled up and climbed the three steps to sit, uneasily, beside me; we listened to water lapping against the floor under our feet. By morning, water had risen to the third step; for a while we wondered what to do, until we looked at the table and figured it would give us some time to think, and then, if we had to swim, we'd have to swim. That's it. All this went on, without a pause, day and all night for what was a long time for us, but the water level stayed about the same, and the wind calmed down at times. I was too nervous even to nap very much. Mostly we sat on the table where the pots and gloves sat along with two Ball bugs and waited for a steady calm.

(Danny recalls that the first of the two off-shore hurricanes appeared late during the month of August that year, so there seems to be some discrepancy as to the time of events occurring here. I pointed out that he might have been thinking of the second of that year's hurricanes, and then, we had to "discuss" the old narrative question of what difference a date makes. Sometimes, disputes over details like this drive an editor crazy. Danny argued that a hurricane is a hurricane and that whichever one it was, or whatever time it occurred, the wild weather brought with it a time of unpleasantness for everyone, and that during this time, whatever time it was, Danny became uneasy because the master didn't want to go outside. No matter what the time or weather, Danny relies upon daily walks to take care of "his business," as he calls it. Of course, to be accurate, Danny himself, as he tells me, loves being wet, but as fate would have it, the Master does not; the Master, even though he can carry an umbrella, does not want to go outside in the rain; it seems he cannot remember where the umbrella is. What can I say? I've come to care less and less about dates and the weather myself; as for umbrellas, though I can gratefully say that I have never in my entire life seen one, in the flesh as one says, I have read about them extensively and know for a fact that they are always lost. E.T.)

For the whole time I've known him, Jake has been more apt to go out rambling into the wet than I am, so during this hurricane time, while he ventured out now and again, I did not and I was becoming hungrier than he. Jake is a good friend to me, he is, but he never was much on bringing back extra portions of food to share. Maybe he figured a mouth like his is too narrow to be able to carry enough food for an extra meal, and maybe it is! Anyhow, even as the water subsided a bit, I found I was not willing to follow behind him seeking out suppers in what to me was still a flood. I spent some time searching out any crickets that might have wanted to use our table as a life raft; I danced off and on some boxes in the shed and chewed their corners, poked at a few leaves floating by the steps, then, finally, did my crouching and waited. There I was, waiting again. This time, I knew what I was waiting for: dry ground and as soon as possible. I looked around at that soggy shed and had a strange thought: some creatures might not want the rain to stop, might be waiting for even more rain and floods to come. Fish for one, I thought.

I did not cry out sadness in front of Jake, but I would think of you when I waited alone in the damp shed, hearing the wind. I'd slip off into a doze with a picture of us kittens sleeping in a bundle together, breathing in our warmth, and I'd see you step into the box, and I could remember and see the three of us start wriggling and calling out for your milk as you would settle down into a curl around us. In my dream, I could feel your spongy belly against my foot pads. Then, I believe I would cry a little and my nose would twitch and I'd wake up with a jump, back where I was, crouching in the shed, empty and cold.

Finally, early one clean fall morning, Jake and I both heard blackbirds and awoke to find the rain had stopped. New sunlight struck every blade of grass with a sparkle of excitement. I stretched and yawned and licked my shoulders twice on each side. We started out early that day, long before dusk, with hopes high, the way they will be when a day you've waited for dawns, a changed day, with its prospects of unknown discoveries.

As I am writing about it now only a short month or so later, I see that the time of the first hurricane did bring about changes, but then I know now that every day brings on discoveries and it remains always to be seen what that means in terms of one's on-going life.

That September morning, not long after the rain stopped, we set out confidently to find a snack, something to tide us over until dark time. If you've never lived like this, Mahrowh, you may not think in terms of the light time as being more fearful than the dark time—well, I mean "the day" as opposed to "the night," to use the Human words. For us, although neither is entirely safe, we find far more dangers around in daylight than darkness. That is life in the city as I discover.

The things I discovered that were called "cars" were a constant problem, along with two-wheeled riders, dogs, other cats, and people, especially children. There's even a bird that Jake had heard about who gets very upset if anything comes as close as 15 opossums to its nest, even by accident, in which case it dive-bombs an attack from above. But we didn't need to worry about that because we knew to avoid daytime. Yes, yes, yes. No daytime for us. As a general rule. But as with any rule, we broke it sometimes, and this time, we did, out of desperation.

Jake headed for a back porch nearby where there was sometimes a bowl of cat food outside the door. I held back at first because it wasn't dark yet, and I could see everything too plainly for my liking. Well, I could tell he'd found food when I heard him crunching away, steady as that falling rain had been, and I lost control; I jumped up right to the edge of the bowl, startling poor Jake, who backed away faster than he usually moved; I shoved my nose in among those pellets, and chewed. I ate noisily with no concern for anyone or anything. I only heard Jake say as he left the porch in a rather undignified manner, tumbling: "Be careful, careful. Watch out. Watch out carefully, that is." I was in no condition to be careful or to watch anything out, starving as I was. Oh, it's true; I could sense movement behind the door, movement and voices, human type voices, but as long as the door stayed shut …Then, with only five or six morsels left in the bowl, I looked up and saw there were two doors, a regular wooden one and a glass one in front of it. The wooden one was open. And sure enough, standing behind the glass door, looking back at me, there they were: two people, a man and a woman. And a rather large yellow dog. Well, who knows what humans can be likely to do, but we all know perfectly well what a dog is likely to do, so

… As quick as one can say "there's no mouse like a live mouse," I left the porch, went onto the ground, and into an opening beside the steps, into a space under the porch. There I was. Hiding and waiting. Crouching in the lonely dark again. I wrote you before about the danger I suspected could be in dark places. What are the chances that all bushes and porches are safe underneath? All right. Looking back again now, I can see that the chances are great they are not all safe. Underneath. And I can see that continuous apprehension will be a stable part of life for the homeless animal, no matter where she ends up, in known or unknown places. She still may have to pounce on those chances, to coin a phrase. And after such a lucky meal, following such a long fast, in the midst of so much apprehension, the chances are a stomach will become nervous. I decide to settle in: I take a deep breath; I do a lickety-split clean-up: I lie down; I think of you, and I fall asleep.

I awake once to the sound of human voices, a lull of sound that I, in half-sleep, connect with the bowl of food on the porch, and I fall back into a dream: a garbage bag, full to bulging with cat food pellets, is sitting right out in plain view on a walkway just like the one near our shed; I leap in delight and land right on top of it; only when I land, I find it has become a wet soggy mess of overcooked noodles, and they will not leave my paw pads. There I am, stuck to the walkway, standing in the middle of a slick, wormy mush. The noodles feel both slippery and sticky to me, to my paws; I hate those feelings; I try to lift each paw clear of the stuff so I can step into the grass and clean it off. But every time I lift up a paw, everything clings to it, stuck in between the pads or dribbling from them like tangled yarn.

I wake up with pricked ears to hear a sort of clicking and bumping sound on the porch. Jake has come back to get me! On second hearing, though, I can tell these snuffling sounds have come down where I hear them just outside the opening to go under the porch, and they are not like Jake's. How can I explain the difference? These snuffles were larger and had a more moisture-filled tone about them; then too, they were very close to the ground, whereas Jake's are an inch or so above it. As I fully awakened, I could use my ears and nose better and soon realized it was the dog I heard and now smelled. I backed away, farther and farther under the porch and, feeling safe enough, began a little exploration of the under-house territory.

Where the porch joined with the house, I found openings, and when I went through, I decided I must be under the room from which voices came. I walked around an area of some 200 dog lengths under the house; I heard water in some pipes overhead and felt heat in others. The floor under the house was quite dry, and there were lots of hopping bugs, fatter than crickets or grasshoppers; I supposed someone might want to catch these. Anywhere I went, I could hear the woman singing, and pretty soon, I heard the man and dog on the porch again, then inside and the man was singing too.

Of course, it did come about that before late dark, I felt hungry again; I roused up a hopping hump bug, but when I ate it, the scent of dirt and mouth full of prickly legs made me sneeze. I thought about Jake coming back, about how we would go out to eat as usual. I wanted to apologize to him for my having been such an impatient glutton about the food on the porch. It's not so pleasant to learn faults about one's self, inner faults, that is, which are not like the random splashes of creamy color all over someone's outer surface. I'd never known how impolite I could be when it came to food.

I did a little introspection, reaching back into my early kittenhood, to explore the origins of this problem. And yes, there I am; I see myself pushing between my brother and sister, head-butting my way to find what I felt was the best place, my own special place; I was aggressive to a fault, and there were only the three of us in the beginning; we all had plenty to drink. But I always wanted the most. Nothing polite or well-mannered there. I mulled certain images over and figured out that my one main weakness had to be food. I'll do anything for it I believe. This could be what I hear of as an "addiction." "Eurrrh." Whatever it is, I fear it will lead me into trouble sometime, as any weakness will. I vowed under that porch, then and there, to make an effort to recover from this problem as soon as I felt safer and could create a more hospitable life circumstance.

Meanwhile, I figured out that self-awareness in itself is an advantage even if it points out faults, because if one takes its revelations to heart, one can benefit from the knowledge; one can change from being an impetuous jumper after food into a careful, aware planner of food procurement.

With that conclusion, I put my new-found awareness to work, crawled back into the porch area and waited, determined not to leap without looking into possible disaster next time. And I thought about how to get more food.

(*Well, Dear Reader, you are probably thinking that Jane is back in the same place as always: waiting and not knowing for what exactly, out of control of her circumstances and not making nearly as much progress as she had when she* had *leapt and reached the food bowl that morning. I can't help but agree with you on this point. Danny, however would like to point out that Jane was still just a kitten, sorting things out, and was, as so many young animals are, full of contradiction and conflict. E.T.*)

After what seemed a long while in stomach time, I crept out of the hole to the base of the stairs—just in time to hear both the back doors open. I saw the woman, and her voice said, "Well, I still say, the little thing must have been awfully hungry to stand off an opossum like that."

I heard her put a bowl down; I heard the doors close; all grew quiet. I found the bowl and almost emptied it before I thought of Jake. I thought of Jake and of how happy he'd be to finish up these pellets. So I waited no longer to set off to find him.

(*Danny continues to let conflicting views about opossums clutter his brain; I, like everyone I know, see the opossum in one way only: as complete scum of the earth. But to go on to the end of the letter … E.T.*)

I do believe I will write again soon. I do believe writing to you gives me new ideas to consider. And lots of old love to remember.

I will remember that love long into the night and remain, your kitten,

Jane

JANE LETTER #5

(Dear Reader, I hope you will excuse another interruption at this point, but I feel it necessary to warn you that the following letter contains an incident that may be disturbing to the quiet sensibilities of some; a reader must not omit at least a quick scanning of this letter however, because its omission might lead to confusion when later plot events unfold. So, while I prepare you to expect dismay, I yet advise you to persevere. E.T.)

My Dear Mahrowh,

Last week when I broke off in the writing of my last letter, I was just setting out to look for Jake, to join him in our nightly search for meals. I especially wanted to make up to him somehow for having been so selfish about the cat food on that previous morning. Even though I wasn't very hungry yet, since the woman had put out another bowl at supper time, I still looked forward to following around after Jake. We had a funny little game we played at times once our initial hunger had been satisfied. Jake would sort out and select a particle of food about the size of his nose and throw it up into the air for me to catch. I got better and better at anticipating the path a particle would take, depending on Jake's nose thrust, and I learned to catch all sorts of food in midair. But Jake was a joker, too: just when I was going along strong, catching everything in sight, he'd toss me a raison or a grape, something he knew I couldn't stand to have in my mouth. Then he'd spread that wide smile of his, and I'd bat a grape or onion right back at him.

When I set out that day it was still pretty early in the evening, maybe 5 or 6 hours after sunset, so I decided to start my search at the shed where we'd been sleeping our days. I could tell he wasn't there even before I looked in his place under the floor. And the scent was old too, by an hour at least. So, I began to trace out the steps of our usual nightly route, starting with the diner. The diner was our first stop because it currently employed a certain kitchen staffer who always left a few garbage can lids half off. And the diner garbage cans were likely to contain the most delicious leftovers, to my way of thinking, in the entire neighborhood, namely, plain ones, that is those of a sort without sauces: for instance, a quarter of a roast beef and cheese sandwich with nothing but bread around it. (Jake told me what this sandwich was called, but at that time, I didn't give a ripe peach seed what its name was!) At least once a week, there was fried chicken. Friday nights and Saturday mornings, we found fish. Good old basic, home-cooked food, as they said on their sign. Excellent. Yes, this food was all on the edible side, unlike that at the Chinese restaurant down the block. There, most times, we couldn't even bear to smell the contents of the garbage cans, even though Jake spent precious moments pulling them out and pushing little things he said were shrimp in my direction. Generally, we couldn't find or separate what might have been meat from the other nameless lumps in there and the whole accumulation was flecked with little red skin patches that would burn holes in your tongue like it was a paper bag. Of course, Jake would eat almost anything, as I've said, but he was good enough to make the "down home" diner his first stop on most nights because of me.

The only trouble was that the diner was on the far side of the street from where our sleeping shed was. That meant we had to cross a major shopping and restaurant road to get there. And that road was something frightening.

I wish you could see a map of the streets where we live and the surrounding area. The wide, crowded street I mention is called Colley Avenue; it runs through the middle of the places we roam and is full of both moving and stationary cars all day and early night, and although in late night there aren't as many moving cars, the ones that are there go faster, faster than necessary, I'd say. The only slight advantage this big street has over the quieter, house-filled streets nearby is that it is brightly lit at night. You can see what's coming and what's coming can see you. But, all in all, if you were to watch us crossing this main street, even in the middle of the night, you would notice our caution. And as I stand at the edge of the curb for a minute, hesitant, I think that, since I am not with him, maybe Jake would have skipped the diner this night. Maybe I could turn back and go to a house we know here on our side. But then, I look up and across, and sure enough, there he is, all of his gray shuffling self; I see him making his way back from the diner, holding close to the building fronts. I follow along across from him on the other side of the street, and I call out to him. I see him turn and begin to cross over to our side, and I call out again. I always gave Jake a little warning about crossing the street. (Well, he does move slowly; everyone, it seems, knows that, and I was always afraid for him. I know it's just his way. And though he can be ferocious when cornered, he's generally a tranquil creature. What is strange is that instead of using those ferocious teeth, he gets signals to roll over at some dangerous times and pretend like he is dead; I had never seen this happen, and I'm even now not sure when he would use this strategy, but he told me quite often that it can work well to deter approaching enemies. Out in the open, I suppose. Before they get too close. I don't know. Some enemies, I suppose, might give up, maybe those other than human ones. But what is a car really? Once a human is in it? Living and not living. An enemy. Thinking and not thinking.)

I see the car coming toward Jake, and this car must see him; it seems to be slowing down for him to cross, slowing down for a moment as he goes slowly … slowly, one little scrappy-nailed foot after the other. Then …

I see the car speed up and swerve and hit Jake.

He is not dead for a while. His legs still walk—as if he will reach the safety of the curb even now. He is so nearly there. I go to him and lick his face; I lick his eyes closed, "addum." And I stay beside him until he has come to his rest.

BOOK I

Part Two

In which Danny reveals, with the assistance of Edith Throckmorton, his reaction to Jake's death, and then gives his version of how Jane arrived and was acclimated to life in his house:

When Danny finished reading this last, short letter, he had to stop and do some careful thinking. For starters, he felt a need to sort out again his very mixed feelings about the creatures he found around him in everyday life, the ones he would like be rid of, the ones he would like to clear off the earth entirely: squirrels and pigeons, no question, rats, the same, but in this case, more specifically, opossums. But then, how to deal with, even more specifically, this particular opossum, Jake, who had all the characteristics of any opossum but who had probably saved the life of the one little creature who meant more to him than any other nonhuman one on the earth. And a particular opossum also, this one, who had met a death that is unnatural and unnecessary and especially painful for any animal, even a human one; he couldn't help but be shocked and offended; he couldn't help but protest such a murder, even if the murdered one had been unknown and completely undesirable to him while alive.

He shook his head. He was thinking these points over, and his mind, out of control, took a turn that brought him to a new awareness. He realized that among the groups of animals he has felt a need to disperse or even dispose of at times are, well, yes, cats, also. But are cats like his adored kitten, Jane, to go in the same category as opossums? Here was a problem. He considered the way he had always curbed his need to destroy when it came to his own cats—first, Maisie; then, Jane—and that's when the new thought came to him: That we can like some things we don't... that we usually don't...like, and that we can stop doing something we usually do if we...if we want to.

> (*This editor is entirely aware of the confused redundancy of Danny's remarks in this section, but Danny was insistent on wording this new idea as he has done so here. We can see that the new idea represents one of the same reasons why he has set these letters out for everyone to read in the first place. In so many words, he says the same thing in his introductory note; now he says it takes a while for the clear truth to sink in, and yet there is nothing clear here yet. Some individuals of some groups, on the whole, may be able to wait for this sort of clarity to arrive, but in my family, there's no such time for endless repeated confusion without action. E.T.*)

Danny went on to consider the fact that, although he never developed a really close relationship with Maisie, he had still refrained from killing and eating her in the presence of the Master and Mistress. For whatever reason. Well, one reason, he determined, was that when he came to the house as a puppy, Maisie was already established there, and first control of a preexisting territory makes for a power position. She had been there some 50 odd cat years and was already full grown. Actually, it occurs to him now that he used to think of her as having always been there in his house and as having always been old. She had an "old" attitude—meaning doing the same things every day and in the same way, slowly and deliberately. Not that we don't all like a little consistency, but variety is also the spice of life, he thought, as he'd heard somewhere and agreed with.

Never mind. All the "thinking" has made him want to lick his parts. *(I think we all find that to be true at times. E.T.)*

Besides, Jane was the first *kitten* he'd known. Unusual and lively in every way to him and a feast for all his senses. When he looked down on her, so small beside him, a little gray storm with puffs of gold all about her, or when he touched her, so soft, his nose would wander about her belly as it sometimes did in the folds of the Mistress's clothes, satin nightgowns or slips. And his tongue would lick and his teeth would gather the folds of her neck or hold her head, carefully, for affection. Even his hard, worn paw pads, even these, reacted with pleasure when they would tumble her about, carefully, very carefully.

But the greatest delight was her odor. His finely tuned dog's nose could appreciate any kind of scent in ways few other creatures can imagine; that's a well-known fact *(and, I fear, also referred to in an earlier passage. E.T.)*, but not all of earth's odors are pleasant; some hit his nose like a rolled up newspaper: weed killer, ammonia, a fact which is not as well known. But the subtle warmth he smelled in Jane's neck made him sigh inside and out. As with any cat, she was clean, of course, but her odor was never bland. She was covered with wonderful licking scents—his own and hers blended—and even inside the house, he could smell the sun and wind on her coat.

When they curled up together, all he could hear was her rough purr and the sound of his tail as it smacked the floor in a regular beat, like the life in a heart. Until they fell asleep.

So. Reading now, he took a breath and thought of how far back that dear sleeping time had been.

He read the letter about Jake's death again. And he thought back in time again, even farther back than the sleeping. He remembered the first time he saw Jane, and that was when Jake was still alive.

That time was after breakfast on a windy day in September, a sunny day, in between the two hurricanes that came that year. It was his walk time, and the Master opened the regular door and was about to open the glass protection door when he turned to Danny and took hold of his collar. Simultaneously, Danny smelled and heard wild animal action on the back porch.

"Calm down now, Dan. Take it easy." The Master is holding him back. Danny is panting hard but does not move. He could take whatever thing it was by the neck, and put it out of its misery in less time than it takes to remove a collar. "Keep sensible," he reminds himself. To the humans, he wanted to look like he was in control, but the truth is he became almost agonized with excitement whenever someone opened the back door, regardless of the day or hour. If someone held his collar, however, the frenzy that he contained internally could only be recognized externally by a slight twitching of nose and ears.

And he loved all the old familiar scents and sounds that came from the porch and yard, all of them, from chair cushions to dew on grass and earthworms to wind chimes and chickadee, dee, dee or the keex, keex of Starling or squirrel, but then, in addition, for Danny, always, the slightest drift of air shifted new scents and sounds up around him, too, every moment—new stimuli for his consideration, odors few other animals could have distinguished: fresh bubble gum from way out on the front sidewalk, scratchings and gnawings, from creatures under rocks and things his humans would not want to notice. Sometimes, he worried that he grew too aroused by this particular door-opening event, that it had become too important to him, the opening of a door! "What's so amazing about that for knuckle-bone's sake! Maybe," he would think, "maybe because the door is combined with the walk itself, the door *opening* has a more extremely powerful effect on me than I would expect. Cuff cuff." He'd always felt, at least he thinks that he'd *often* felt, that it isn't really natural for a healthy dog to be held back, for instance, behind a closed door when everyone else is on the other side, or on the floor beside a table when there's a meal ready to be eaten on top, but as he grew older, he'd learned that a dog could do well if he kept in control of himself, behaving the way those around him indicated, thereby receiving treats and such on a regular basis, and exactly unlike the terrier on the next street over who was always being struck on the head with his own leash handle. Sometimes he thinks that such a controlled behavior could be normal for his certain breed of dog, but in the long run, he has come to think that it is nothing more than the way he has been trained, in the presence of treats and such, for years. All that being said, at times he still feels confused about why he does certain things.

(And who wouldn't be confused after going through all the stages of confusion, after all the "I used to think this" and "then I thought that" and "now I might think something else." I have tried to convince Danny to restrict or even eliminate entirely these thoughtful ruminations; I have pointed out that the reader may become confused, too, as he did. I did not mention that a reader might become bored as well. Really, Danny has such a good-natured, honest way of opening up to his thoughts that I don't like to hurt his feelings, so, in the end when he told me he thinks the readers need to know his mood and state of mind as he goes into the next part of his story, I had to go along. Sometimes one has to go along. And sometimes I am thankful for a relatively small, compact brain size. E.T.)

On the morning in question, the scraping sounds and opossum scent mixed together with the scent of seasoned cat food have an almost mesmerizing effect on Danny, and he is relieved, at least temporarily, when the Master pulls back on the collar and gives the "sit and stay" command.

"Be quiet, Danny, now." The Master speaks in a low voice. "Sal, come over here. Look at this. There's an opossum on the porch. Eating your cat food."

"At nine o'clock in the morning? That's strange." The Mistress comes to look. "He must be really hungry."

"I remember suggesting that you not leave extra cat food on the porch."

The Mistress had a bad habit of leaving extra cat food outside in case someone out there got hungry. Danny didn't think she cared who it was that might be hungry, and so the Master worried about various diseases that animals can bring into the yard, especially the cat next door. (*Note: Danny may not be referring to the black cat that was mentioned earlier. There may be another cat involved. I have made a note to check on this detail. E.T.*) That cat's family wouldn't let him live in the house, and sometimes, he ran out of food. But the world includes lots of creatures looking for handouts; any meal left outside is up for grabs. If he thought of it at all, Danny himself did not think it would be a good idea to live out on the sidewalk, hoping that food would appear sometime in the driveway.

> (*This last remark provides a new insight into Danny Lunder's background: the fact that he lacks a broad liberal education reflects like grease in a frying pan when he implies he might have had a choice about his living situations. I don't think so. Not after 30 thousand years of domestication. E.T.*)

Meanwhile, at the back door, Danny's rear end has scooted just a tick's length or two forward, and at about that point, he lifts out of the sit-and-stay position and moves slowly to the door himself, his tongue half out of his mouth. He sees it all: The three of them watch: the opossum is crunching away on the dry cat food; there's a sudden gray movement; a shadow slides, skidding into the side of the food bowl and begins sucking up cat pellets like a dust buster, about a pound a minute. Everyone behind the door holds still for a suspenseful three seconds or so, until, as they look on, that opossum backs away, one, two, three steps, just like that and tumbles off down the porch steps. The little cat never raises a whisker, just goes right on swallowing everything whole. Just like that. As Danny watches, his tongue slides back into position, but his lips tremble; he is about to explode; the Master could be feeling Danny's energy boiling strong because he reaches down and secures the collar again. They watch some more.

"Wow. I never would have thought a kitten could stand off an opossum like that. They must both be really hungry." Danny had long since learned that the Mistress could be fascinated by any behavior having to do with any kind of living thing.

"Well, that's no good reason for leaving food out on the porch all the time. It'll attract too many problematic animals and cause all sorts of … problems in the long run."

"Hunger?" The Mistress had her ways of talking.

"You know what I mean."

That the Master was cautious when it came to all animals but dogs, Danny had learned, too, also by observation. Meanwhile, on the porch, the kitten was finishing up; there was a little pause, and then, the Master hooked on Danny's leash and opened the glass door. The kitten had disappeared.

"Just as well," Danny thought at that point. "One cat is more than enough cat for me. As far as problems go."

The rest of the morning had gone along pretty much as usual—the walk the same as most days, the same turn halfway around the block into the vacant lot that is used for team sports by the elementary school children, a few minutes running in the grass there, the Master picking up the feces Danny usually places beside the left soccer goal post, then with the leash back on, finishing off the rest of the block home. Basically, this daily walk must have looked boring to someone like a human, seeing it day after day, but Danny was not bored by the sameness of his walks; he looked forward to reconnecting with the same old familiar odors day in and day out, feeling that sense of continuity, security, but of course, as one can imagine, he also greatly welcomed the unpredictable whiffs of new things, and he got them frequently enough to brighten his life considerably: scenting a new squirrel in the neighborhood or old one with a new baby or acorn was a treat even if he never saw them; just keeping track of everyone's travels, in and around the area, was good fun. Human odors, of course, were often new, but to be honest, he wasn't as interested in those as, well, of course, as in the squirrels' and rats', opossums', raccoons', and, to a lesser extent, the pigeons', doves', and random birds'. The best was the scent of a new dog, and a female dog's scent topped the list of excitement, as any male would know. All new scents were a delight for him, and there were bound to be a few every day. So, one can see why the walk was the center of his life.

When he thought of the walk that day as uneventful, however, he was making a distinction; he was thinking of the kind of event in which he caught a scent—a new scent, a fresh one—all at once, all around him, and then turned to smell it attached to its owner right there, near enough that he could see the form and shape, even (depending on the leash) touch the scent maker with his nose ... Well, that was the tops, the full blast of excitement: the odor, the sight, the touch combined—all the very reality of the thing itself. And the fast hot sensation he felt by that kind of experience was eventful indeed, not something that happened every day, on every walk.

He had almost caught a squirrel once. It all began when he'd been sniffing, slowly and quietly for once, back and forth, in a damp boarder along his front sidewalk. It had been worked by a pair of Robins just before he'd arrived. As he snuffled into the moist earth, he caught a side drift of squirrel, a Clamper's scent it was; that is the scent of a young squirrel, newly out of the nest, much like himself in age. He turned and plunged headlong into the large camellia bush at the corner of the driveway. On the ground underneath, long unraked, old bush and flowers leaves lay in rag piles, hills and valleys that the baby squirrel's nose and paws were exploring, were actually scattering flat, at a fierce rate. Danny surprised the squirrel while its face was in a valley; he got there just in time to pounce on and hold down that brand new fuzzy tail; the fresh, warm reality of its movement made him yelp with excitement. Then, he forgot to stabilize the tail with his front feet or his back feet (He wouldn't have known which to use anyway.) before he reached for the neck. A turmoil resulted.

Danny has never been sure whether the leash became entangled in the bush branches for a moment or whether the Master had secured the leash himself by that time, but it stopped him and he stood panting with disappointment. Since then, he has never yet come as close to catching a prey, but that one event left him with a little twitching hope that someday, on some walk, something like that could happen again.

Anyway, as he thinks back on those first meetings with Jane, he remembers that he had not seen the kitten when they finished the walk that first meeting day, nor, it seems to him, does he remember seeing it for several days following.

Nevertheless, the Mistress continued to put food outside on the porch.

And one morning, in the days after that first morning, she left the wooden door open and Danny and she watched as the kitten came up to eat its fill. Well, Danny found himself wiggling all over with the anticipated pleasure of actually contacting this new creature, the thought that he might have that opportunity very soon, at any moment now. From around the door edges, he could scent that it was a very young cat and a female and, as such, of absolutely no threat to him at all, none at all. After a while he sat back, his nose dripping with the wondrous new kitten scents and his eyes glued to the tiny little body, its throat and belly moving softly with the pellets as they moved along; she was so close to him, there, with the Mistress, on his porch.

Danny was not as completely pleased, however, as the days went on. The Mistress began spending lots of time outside on the porch, and she served the cat special canned food along with the dry pellets as often as four times a day. Well, Danny himself was lucky to eat once in 24 hours; if he received anything extra, in the way of a snack or treat, it was unpredictable; no, usually he had to be content with one large meal a day at supper. This has never seemed fair to him. Never. Maisie had her food left out all the time, but he couldn't reach it. These multiple feedings, for any reason, for other animals did not sit well with him. But since the Mistress often left the inner door open when she fed the kitten, Danny got to look out more often, and he did enjoy watching the activity outside.

He watched as the Mistress moved the food bowl closer and closer to the door, as she moved it closer to where she sat for long moments with her hand out, not moving, by the food. And he watched as one day, the Mistress began rubbing the kitten's head as it ate.

"Anyone enjoys a good scratch on the head," he thought, remembering how he could sit for hours by the chair while the Master worked, sit for hours just to gain a minute or two of being scruffed up. "Just don't *pat* me," he thought. Maisie says she can take it or leave it as far as scratching goes, but she sure as paper crackles won't wait hours for it, and she'll walk away in the middle of it. But who knows if Maisie sets the standard for all cats. And meanwhile there was the new one to wonder about. During the feeding operations, it was quiet outside on the porch and inside, too for Danny; and, sometimes, as he sat alone behind the glass door, he even thought he could hear the kitten purr.

All of this activity did not go unnoticed by the Master: "I see you have chosen to disregard my advice about the food on the porch," he said one day.

"Usually, I put it out only during the daytime now, and I sit there while it's out."

"You sit out there and feed that cat. You admire that cat. You want to help it. You most likely have a plan."

This sort of thing has happened before it seems, but Danny can't remember; he wonders about everything that went on before he arrived.

"Well, nobody's going to adopt a cat that's half wild and skinny as a knitting needle. You know. My plan," she said, "is to feed it up, get its shots, get it neutered, and take it to the Animal Assistance League; they don't put anyone to sleep there. I admit that sometimes you have to wait a long time until there's a space."

"I know that plan."

"And I've carried it out before. Don't get nervous. I can do it again."

There was a pause as we all thought about the future.

"Is it a male or female?"

"I'd think a male, given the aggressive personality. No offense meant."

"It's a strange looking cat."

"Do you think so?" The Mistress didn't sound very enthusiastic about the appearance of the cat. "It's kind of messy looking. All those irregular streaks and spots of yellow creamy colors, one falling from its chin like a goatee."

"There's a small spot under its right eye, like a tear. Gives it a curiously melancholy look."

"So, that's good. Maybe someone will fall in love with that look."

"Umm."

Danny could tell that the Master was wondering who would do that.

As he read the letters, as he recalled all these important events, Danny had to recall how negative the Master's first feelings were toward the kitten. (Only later did they call her Jane.) He remembered how much he, himself, used to dislike cats, too. He pawed through the remaining letters and wondered how many of his and the Mistress's and even the Master's regular conclusions about life had changed because of Jane, and how many others he, himself, might have to change in the future because of reading her letters, and he was tempted to lay them aside.

(Danny is honest enough that he wishes me to inform the reader of his reservations about continuing to read Jane's letters. I have put the following section in his own voice. E.T.)

Dear Reader:

When I reached this place in the reading of Jane's letters, I have to tell you I felt like stopping. Do you remember what Jane wrote about how she felt when she first began writing the letters, when they were bringing her terrible sad memories and feelings. Well, I here am now learning things that are ruining lots of ideas it has taken me 20 dog years or more to get straight. These letters have already upset me, and I am only part way through. And now, I am considering how many more ideas might be ruined or disturbed by reading any more letters. Well, as you can see, I did not let my fears prevail, or these letters would not be in your hands today, obviously. (*Obviously*.) But to look back...No. What I did was to look forward. I shuffled the pages and looked at the next letter. And, of all things, as if it was a sign or a message, the next letter was Jane's version of how she first met me! And I couldn't just put it down and wait for some other time or decide not to find out how she felt. Don't we all want to know how others see us? Who doesn't like listening behind a door? So, I hope you will excuse me for thinking only of myself in those few deciding moments because, in the end, you will also have the excitement of meeting me again, too!

JANE LETTER #6

Dear Mahrowh,

I have been thinking about Jake and the night he died, and it seems to me, looking back, that you must have seen times of death too. Of one time I remember: the little boy and the little girl with my name, Jane, carried my brother Tippy up the stairs and back down, and they were both trying to hold onto him so that they fell and Tippy was howling and they took him away, as you said, to *"The Vet"* and he never came back. Now, I think that he must have died; I had never thought about it at all, not at all, then, about what had really happened or about how you must have felt. Well, I had never heard about death then.

I stayed beside Jake for a long time. My eyes went over and over along his gray face, up from his fine nose to his tiny ears, down to his funny long tail. After a while, when I couldn't feel any more, I moved away; I'm not sure which way. Later, I went back to the shed, into the window, and found the crate I usually slept in, but you can imagine how silent it was without Jake underneath. When the dark time came again, and I was still alone then, I went back to the house where the woman left food out on the porch.

(Danny made a mistake about his part of the story being found in this letter. It's one of the next letters that is about him. There is a meeting in this letter, however, so you may as well read on. E.T.)

Sure enough, the food was there, and I thought of Jake as I ate it, of how strongly he enjoyed a good meal, of how much he liked me to enjoy one, too, and of the way he always allowed me to eat whatever was left when he had finished, or even, I thought with a little pang of guilt, when he hadn't. I knew he would want me to finish this food, but just then I heard a voice from outside my head:

"That's my food. Pull yourself back, now."

I jumped to run, turning, and I saw a large orange cat with one crossed eye and ears that looked like they'd been caught in a can opener.

"That's my food." He spoke again and his words sounded as if they were being dragged through a thick bean soup. Despite the claiming words, his feet just stood still, so mine did too.

"That's my food," he said for the third time, "and I get it every day." He looked at me (or at least it seemed like he might be looking at me, for it's hard to tell with a cross-eyed creature). I considered what to reply. Although he hadn't exactly asked a question, he seemed to be in want of a response.

"Well," I said, "I surely would not normally eat another cat's food, but since I have none of my own, I wonder if you would consider sharing, just this one time? Besides, I really think the lady puts it out for me now too. She knows I'm here."

"Oh, she does, does she? Oh, you think she does, do you?" And he took a couple of steps toward me, his belly swinging in a cat-door flap; he was definitely not at starvation's door. He eased an abundant rear end down to the floor and pushed his ears stiff back.

"On the other hand, I can easily leave for the time being," I said, but I didn't leave, maybe backed up a step. I held my ground. Judging from the way he spoke and the way he had approached me so far, I figured this cat would probably move with the speed of a snail through salt.

"Well, that's the way it is, is it?" There was a long pause while he may have gathered his thoughts together. "I see."

I waited.

"You could try hunting, you know. You're young and hardy."

"What?"

"Crickets are moving slow this time of year."

"What?"

"Those black things, pop up and down … Crickets. Crispy. You know."

"Oh," I said. "Oh… And you eat them?"

"Does a dog eat– never mind."

"They're pretty small."

"Well, sure they are; you have to– never mind. That's the way it is then." He scratched the left ear, rather roughly, I think, then shook his head and finally went on to say, "Never mind, little gal. You just go ahead and help yourself to my overflowing pellet food bowl right now. I can wait. Should be watching my weight anyways." He gave a big laugh, which turned into a cough. "I get more than plenty regular meals next door, you know. Shoot, they're pretty good to me over there. It's a pretty good area around here. Yep, and last spring there was a bunch of us… never mind. I'm just not getting any younger, you know. Last spring … Did I say that? Whoa, moahougha. Well, there must have been 5, 6 of us fellows and then came along such a real comely little calico. Haven't been the same since. I want to say it's all been worth it, all the springtime revels over the years, so I will say that, but I'm slowing down, cricketwise. Oh, I still get into the shuffle, especially now all the neighbors are helping me out, but I look around, and I don't see my yellow-orange colors sprinkling the landscape like they used to." He gave me a sideways look. "You aren't … um …? How old are you, honey?"

"I'm still a baby," I said, but it was as if he hadn't heard me at all.

"All that tomfoolery."

(I was back at the food bowl by this time, crunching away.)

"A lover and a fighter. Always have been. All my life. It's wrecked my brain. Can't even tell when a little gal's coming of age anymore. Wrecked my nose."

I looked up at his ears, too, as his eyes peered off into the past.

"Used to be, in the old days, over the old years, 'foot-loose and fancy free,' as the humans say, I built up quite a reputation, quite a following, you know, around the neighborhood. Handouts all over the place. 'Course I was better lookin' then. And full of spunk."

All was quiet on the porch. He stared over in the vague direction of the house next door and scratched at a fur mat on his neck.

"Nowadays, it's pretty much come down to the two places you see here. This one and that over there. I don't go inside over there, but I could if I wanted to. A dog's inside over here."

"I know."

"You're small."

"I know."

"Well then, eat up, my little Night Eyes. Savor those pellets. Put some shine on that funny lookin' gray and splotchy coat, some meat on them scrawny rib bones. A bird under the paw, as they say."

"I'd be glad to share with you now."

"Just you don't trouble yourself on my account now. All that struggling around for grub's a thing of the past for me, traipsing around trash cans, seeking out all the old cold and stinkin' places connected with food and freedom. Shoot! That stuff can pull an animal down. You get to smelling bad too, for one thing. I was not raised to be a bum. My mum had circus plans for me. But that's another long story. And what mum doesn't, for that matter. She provided me with a decent family, human father, human mother, kids, goldfish, the whole shebang. Just not my thing, not my thing. So, I took off. Well, and what Tom wouldn't for that matter. Then, like I say, last spring took place ... Hmm? And now this hurricane weather's making my joints ache like I'd landed down from some attic window."

He sat for a moment, staring here and there, then licked, two strokes and three, his left front leg.

"I always liked humans, though, on ground level," he went on, "the way you don't have to do much with 'em, just wrap around the legs, and there's the pellets and "hold up your chin," there's the scratch and rub. Well, I was pretty beat up and tired after that little calico. Anyway, the people next door made me an offer I couldn't refuse, if you get my meaning. Dependable food—the dry pellets sitting out all the time, all the time, and then the canned out every night, regular as clockwork. Naturally, there were tradeoffs."

He showed me his neck then, turned to the side so I could see more closely: a name tag and a bell dangling from a metal circle on a thing he later told me was a collar, a pink collar. I moved around so

I could see from another angle and again considered what to say, not wanting to appear forward but curious about the apparatus itself.

"Well." I took a little pause. "How does that feel," I finally asked, "clamping onto your neck, I mean?"

"Tight." He says. "And then there's the color. They're good folks over there, but I don't think they, uh, I don't think they know much about my true nature."

I didn't either, of course.

"But enough about me, little lady. It's a warm night …Shoot, I can show you the sights. Take you to some different porches, to a few garbage bins only I know about. There's an all-night convenience store a couple blocks down."

Well, those suggestions brought back pretty many sad memories; I hardly knew what to say. "I thank you anyway, but I have a good friend who knows all the restaurants … That is …" I was going to tell him about Jake before I remembered. "I think I'll be all right. This bowl was plenty full for a small cat."

"You bet! Listen, I could show you my day sleeping-nook; it's not so far away, nice and warm …?"

"That's very kind of you, really it is, but I … I did have a place, too, in an old garden shed…" And right then I remembered: the loneliness. So I was just about to take him up on the warm sleeping place offer when the lady who had falsely called out "kitty, kitty" to me appeared on the porch next door. I turned to my yellow neighbor: "I think maybe I'll stay under a bush for now; that lady of yours over there doesn't like me a bit. But I thank you anyway."

"Oh. Yeah. Same old story. Well, if you need anything, just call me over, just call out to me."

"I will do that. I will call out …?"

"Yep, you just call right out."

"What do I call out, then, Yep? Is that your name?"

"My name. My name? What name?"

"For me to call out. Yep? Is that what they call you by? When they call you to dinner, for instance. Yep?"

"Well, yep, they do make a noise. They sure do make a noise; it's that 'kitty, kitty' one."

"I've heard that noise."

"So, I think that's it. Yep, I think that's what they call me."

But right at that moment the lady over there starts calling, "kitty, kitty, kitty."

I thanked him again for the meal and headed off the porch and under a bush, out of sight and alone.

"Kitty, Kitty, Kitty." I was feeling unusually full by then, of food in my belly and sadness everywhere else. I was thinking of being without a name and then of being without someone who would call my name, of having no one like you, Mahrowh, or Jake, who knows me and calls my name.

Maybe it doesn't matter to everyone whether we're all called the same or if we have our own separate names, but tonight I say, it does matter to me.

As ever, I am your loving kitten, called,

Jane

JANE LETTER #7

My Dear Mahrowh,

The mind must badly need to forget some of the bad things that happen to it or it would be so sad it would send us into our hunch and crouching position for good. I had thought I would feel close to Jake and comfortable staying in the place where we had lived together, but every morning when I checked back there, all the old times and good feelings came to meet me at the window like so many hungry pigeons, begging me to come inside when they know very well I could not breathe, could not move, under their wings any more than I could fly away. So, I see now that it was not just convenience that led me to take up sleeping under the porch of the house where the dog lived. Of course, the food was excellent, but I also see now there were other incentives, one of which was the presence of company and the touch of other creatures.

The woman who put the food out talked to me; she spoke the whole time I ate. Her voice reminded me of the little girl I was named for at my birth house during the times that little girl was quiet and soft in her manner, the times she put me with her dolls in the cradle and told stories and sang songs. This new woman sat with me on the porch, closer and closer each time she put the food out. Then, one day, she touched me just on top of my head beside my ear and, then, in front of my ear in places that always need rubbing, places that can be hard to reach with the back legs. Naturally, I leaned in toward her fingers and felt my purr arise.

"Little gray kitten, little brave, stormy-cloud-covered kitten … You must have had a person for a friend once. Isn't that right?"

That word "person" aroused some misgivings inside me. I wasn't sure where I had heard it. I made a small "ahrouh" sound and moved about a dog's length away. As I looked at her carefully, I realized, I believe for the first time, that the humans don't always understand what we say to them; even the little girl with my name, perhaps didn't. I looked at this one for a long time and found that as long as I looked directly at her or sat within a close distance of her, I could understand her words well enough even though she only partly seemed to understand mine. I am recording hers here. But who knows for sure if I have them down correctly? Maybe we can never hear for sure or ever know all that we should about other creatures, even ourselves …or what we can hope for.

But we can know enough to keep on trying.

And before long, we find enough love in the air to pull some back with us under our bushes or porches, fold it close up, warm around our chins, comfort against unknown dangers. When we curl up and close our eyes.

Your comforted kitten,
Jane

BOOK 1

Part Three

A narrator's digression: Danny wants to explain his own communication theories, which boil down to his idea that dogs understand more of Human than do cats, and that dogs, in addition, do not have to be near the person talking to understand what is being said. In addition even to that (canine-centered) idea, Danny also believes that humans understand more of Dog than they do of Cat. He thinks dogs pay closer attention to humans than cats do. He says that if Jane had really paid attention instead of moving, as she says, "a dog's length" away, both she and the Mistress might have understood each other better.

I myself, an antennae-touching insect, have a very hard time caring about oral communications of any kind, but especially those between cats and humans. So, Dear Reader, you can imagine how much I am not pleased to include the following section of Danny's seemingly endless digression on his interpretation of the phrase "a dog's length." Danny is not at his best when trying to explain these dog measurements, but he looks down with that eagerly open-eyed inquiry and that panting-tongue smile he does, and sometimes it's just impossible to argue against him. It is not impossible for me to suggest, however, that the reader may wish to skip this segment of the story entirely. E.T.

First of all: what is "a dog's length"?

- Initially, he thought it to be an expression that refers to a certain dog; that is, a dog that is familiar to the listener or reader; in this case, "a" dog's length would be the length of Danny himself because he is the only dog nearby. But then, he remembered that "a" could refer to any dog in the world; then he remembered that he wasn't even there on the porch when the fear occurred; "a dog" could have meant the Yorkshire terrier the next block over. No. No. No. Jane had never even seen that terrier.
- So he considered the fact that dogs come in different sizes. And what would be the point of being a Yorkshire terrier or Pomeranian's distance away from something very dangerous?
- He then thought the meaning could vary depending on the nature of the danger. If you were near something very dangerous, you'd want to be a Great Dane's length away, but if the danger was minimal, well, the terrier or Pom's length might be okay.
- But then, in that case, if the amount of danger was indicated by the size of dog, shouldn't the expression refer to a specific breed of dog since that's the only way to make the size really clear? And that way you would have a better idea of just how big or small a danger was by knowing the exact length of distance you should move away, toy poodle or St. Bernard.
- He then imagined, in a flash of inspiration, that the expression could refer to a certain, monstrously large, hypothetical god-like dog that would always be used to indicate a safe distance away from any dangerous object or person or creature, a sort of "whale-sized"

mythological, maybe fire-breathing, dog, whose feats of protection have been passed down for generations! Why not something like that?

- Finally, when he thinks his brain will split like a dropped pumpkin, he decides that "a dog's length" is a weak and vague and meaningless and indeterminate expression, any way you look at it and useless for any one except a cat.

("Ditto" and "Hurrah," I said when I finally finished typing this section. I wondered if Danny was miffed as he went on and on about it because the truth is that the dog measurement expression certainly could have been referring to him even if he had not been on the porch at the time because he was ... Never mind. Of course, later, we may well find out what the words mean, to Jane at least, and then, I suppose, I will have had to type all of that explanation as well. E.T.)

JANE LETTER #8

In which Jane, finally, gives her version of coming into the house where Danny lives and meeting its inhabitants, including (this time without a doubt) Danny Lunder himself:

Dear Mahrowh,

As the meals go on, not to mention the days, I have stopped living under the porch except at night. And during the days, I've been happy as a June cricket, bouncing around in and about the small yard that surrounds the porch. When I'm not out there batting October crickets now, I can stimulate action in little balls and fuzzy things the woman throws down the walkway that leads to the garbage can. Sometimes, I stop and see that garbage can and feel a little soft vibration, a little silent purring inside; sometimes I wonder what is in there today. But then, I wander up on the porch and cat-nap on a wonderfully squishy towel (or is it a blanket?) my woman has put in a box under one of the porch chairs.

> *(I forgot to confirm with Danny, but I assume that Jane did not know the difference between a towel and a blanket at this time. E.T.)*

I go up to greet this woman whenever she leaves the door, and she greets me back. I watch closely the dog that sits and waits inside, behind the door; the way his nose and ears move intrigues me. The ears are large and thick, and, unlike mine, they fall downward to the sides. Even so, they have movements about them that set off my attack notions.

Later:

Yesterday, we had a terrible rain again and wind that blew down the wind chimes. (*This was the second off-shore hurricane of that fall. E.T.*) I trembled under the porch during the night; the sounds all around were fearful—cracking and whirring. In the morning, I heard the door open and I rushed out and up as fast as I could, hoping not to be blown away, arriving on the porch just in time to see my woman open the door and put the food dish down, not outside near the door, but inside near the door. Everything shook as the wind pushed in all directions, and then, in a gust, blew me across the door sill; I think it was the wind, but I remember I did not place my feet out in front to stop me. The room was not wet or windy; it was warm and dry and bright with light. The floor was so smooth and clean I slipped and skidded head long into my food bowl. The woman laughed at first, when some of the pellets flew out, but then she stroked my neck as I ate and spoke to me in a low soft voice; as I licked up the last of the canned tuna (I think it was) and pellets, I looked up at her mouth:

"What a good cat, such a fine lady, a little stormy-weather gal." The woman scratched my back, nice and hard.

It wasn't long before the large yellow dog approached the table and licked up the stay food. He was polite, very cautious, because the woman told him to be. After eating, he touched my nose with his, then snapped back as if he feared I would swipe him with my claws out. But I guess I reserve most of my aggression for incidents involving food. So, in a moment, he sidled his way over, and, as it is with dogs, he went about sniffing all over me, and really, I felt myself getting damp and sticky with cat food from the floor. I thought I'd move away, but the nose was big. Well, he finished one round and started in another, and I was just about to make a serious protest when about midway into the second shift, he began to lick my fur down and with such powerful swipes of conviction and love that a motor-like purring erupted from me—outside my control.

That dog went over and over me, back and back with a tongue as large as my head and neck put together, and I felt myself being moved along the floor backwards, toward the door. The woman was laughing.

"Jack, come and see this scene," she called out. "And listen to it too."

"They seem to be getting along almost too well," the man said. "What a loud purr. Are you sure she's not going to be hurt? Danny could swallow her in one mouthful."

"Oh, no. Not her. Not this stormy-weather lady. Look at her! Having survived we don't know what out there in the world, dealing with a dog 20 times her size."

"At least. Well, and then there'll be Maisie to deal with. Hmm?"

"I had forgotten Maisie for the moment. She won't want a housemate."

But I was being pushed too near the door, a place I didn't want to be, and so at that moment, I just took off. I figured I'd find another place, a place to hide, away from all doors and porches.

As you well know, Mah, one should always, even in open and seemingly safe situations—or *especially* in those situations—have a place high enough or low enough that one can't be reached. Isn't that the cat's truth?!

I knew the dog would follow me; I knew I didn't know my way around either, but I also saw, thanks to you, Mah, and our other house, all sorts of structures—you know, furniture, sitting about the rooms, most with spaces under them, between them, on top of them. Ideally, what one wants is a space at least double cat length and just wide enough to turn around in, to face the outside world with claws positioned and ready. Not that I'd attack this dog on such short acquaintance, but I'd had such an eventful last hour that I needed some privacy, and the truth is, I did also need to clean the dog lickings off, restore myself to normalcy of odor. I later came to tolerate, even to like, smelling the dog's tongue, but that was a gradual process.

I found a cozy place in a small room under a small kind of seating furniture (called, I learned later, a "love seat"). It was larger than a chair but smaller than a sofa; its main appeal for me was a colorful flowered cloth that hung down low in the front, almost touching the floor, and behind that, several neatly arranged piles of books that provided corridors and barriers, like little streets and buildings I could go around and behind, to stay out of sight. But when necessary, I could see under the front cloth just enough to keep in touch.

I had no sooner found the love seat than the dog found me. He just lay down and put his nose between his paws and watched me as best he could from in front of the flowered cloth. I washed myself to the sound of dog tail flopping, a regular *pattern*—plop and plop—against the rug, a gentle sound, almost hypnotic in its effect, as peaceful as the rain on Jake's and my old shed. As the days went on, this same sound put me to sleep time and time again. Like the rain or your sweet purr, Mah, it became one of the greatest comforts in my life to me.

And so those sleepy sounds brought about a deep rest for …

Your safe kitten,
Jane

(*Danny says he doesn't remember ever seeing Jane write any letters. [Well, of course he doesn't because he didn't even know she had written any.] He thinks it must have been some time after she'd been living in the house a while and that she may have forgotten some of the details about her arrival. He expects to say more about that later. Meanwhile, I am directed to tell you that he also doesn't remember Jane ever telling him how comforting the sound of his tail was to her and that if he had known, he would have kept it going a lot more. When he speaks of that time and when he describes Jane as she was then, he often makes some soft little whimpering sounds. They aren't exactly sad sounds, I'd say, but nostalgic. As for me, the flopping tail of a dog could kill. Say no more. E.T.*)

JANE LETTER #9

My Dear Mahrowh,

I've been trying to remember some of these early events ... I thought I was napping under the love seat for a fairly long while before the woman came to check on me, but maybe it was only a minute or two. You know how we cats can catch a good, solid rest in only a few minutes, then stretch out ready for the next thing!

I felt sorry for the woman because I could tell she must have been looking under everything in the house to find me. I could tell by her voice.

"Well, there you are!" She sounded greatly relieved, as if I might have disappeared somehow when she was looking under something else. I wonder if you felt that way when Boots and I disappeared without warning. My new human sounded just like you always did, Mahrowh, in your motherly way, always encouraging me to think good things about my efforts. "What a smart girl you are! You've found one of the best places for seclusion in the whole house. I guess it's been a special day for you, little brave girl, and you must need your rest. I expect it's hard to fall into an undisturbed sleep out there in the uncertain backyards and streets."

I felt my purr begin as she talked—because of her connection with food, I suppose, but maybe other things as well—and my paws and claws moved down and up, in and out; I was feeling so easy and relaxed.

She said, "If we all would purr like that, we could never dislike each other." She went away quietly, without trying to pull me out at all, and then, I believe I did sleep for a long time.

When I woke up, the dog was still there. I could sense his presence even though the tail was now still. I concluded that he had gone to sleep as I had. I could see part of his nose, large, blocking the light, so I put my head out beneath the front cloth just a bit, to smell it and feel it, "only a nose throw away," you might say: cold and damp...rubbery. Twitch. I saw it twitch. He was beginning to smell me in his sleep. That was fun. More twitching. Maybe he was dreaming of chasing me up a chair. I reached out my right paw, claws retracted, and carefully touched his nose. With a final large twitch, he jerked awake and pulled back onto the rug, as did I under the cloth. Then, he slid forward to place his nose down close to the area where I was and made a little sound, a wet snuffling sound that reminded me somehow of Jake. The nose stayed there a long time; I grew impatient, and finally, I touched it again. He made a low "ruff" kind of bark. That is a BIG mouth. I pushed my way farther back under the love seat, and there we were, silent, if you can imagine.

Then he said, "Cloudy kitten."

"Jane," I replied, so surprised, I could hardly say a word back.

"This is Danny out here," he said. "I'm the dog that ... the dog that you've been seeing, here ... and out there ... outside on the porch, for one place and then ... inside too ..."

I gathered from the way he stumbled in speech that he must have been shy when meeting new creatures, but then later, I realized that because he and the one they called Maisie were not close friends, he'd had few opportunities to practice conversational Cat. And although most of us creatures can understand each other on the basic level of ordinary polite exchange: the weather, nearby dangers, etc., our different dialects and unique species words make some subtle communications pretty near impossible. Do you remember how that little dog who lived in our first house used to try and talk to us about obeying the Mistress and Master and how we just never could understand what he meant? Of course, he was yipping away, interrupting himself almost constantly, and then, because he was scared to death of you, Mah, that little guy had to keep a good-sized dog's distance away, all of which made it hard to concentrate on what he was saying.

The Danny here at this house is a very different style of dog; although he is large, he speaks quietly and moves more slowly than that other one. I put my head out and we touched noses again.

Then, I had a chance to sniff around his head, the most wonderful part being his soft, padded ears that fall down near enough for me to rub against.

"I did know a dog once," I told him, by way of opening up a conversation, "even talked to him some, but I never got close enough to feel his ears. My mother was fierce when it came to keeping that dog away from us kittens."

"That sounds like a good mother."

Even the dog has made me think of you, Mah, of our first days, and I had trouble listening for a bit.

"I think I would recognize my mother," he said, "if I smelled her, but I'm not sure of it."

"Well, and our mother got very nervous, you can imagine, as we grew older and started chasing this dog around, you know, the way kittens will do. The people had to put him in the pantry at night. And during the day, he was as good as a cat at finding places to hide, so, really, we never got to know him. I bet he was glad when we were taken away." I had never thought of that before…

"Sometimes, I hide from Maisie," Danny said.

The talk of hiding and mothers sent me into a strange mood. I noticed I had almost left the flowered cloth behind and stood out on the rug with only a drift of cloth over the end of my tail. And I was looking hard at the rest of the room, thinking to catch sight of extra hiding places. Meanwhile, the dog, Danny, lifted his body, in lumps, as if a potato sack were rising and stood up beside me; his tail swung back and forth like a human making fan wind, and he said, "Come on." And he took me around all over that house! But all this newness has worn me out right now, so I'll stop this letter and start another one, full of new and unusual (and even some usual) events, on a new and brightly encouraging other day.

Your now grateful home-body,

Jane

JANE LETTER #10

A letter in which Jane tells of her first meeting with the infamous Maisie and all that that involved:

Dear Mahrowh,

My first hours in the house were with the woman and Danny, the man, and, finally, the cat that they had spoken of, and they were just what you would expect; being a part of life itself as they were, they consisted of some moments of joy and comfort, some of fear and foreboding, one of actual pain, and many of just plain being around.

The pain came along my way as the last creature of the house did—that is, when Maisie came along my way. Well, I had sensed that there was another cat somewhere in the house even before they all mentioned her. As you know, we are aware of the presence of strange creatures around us even when we can't see them; we can't always tell what they are or what they'll do, however, so all of us end up having to take our chances with each other.

And sure enough, just as Danny and I were getting to know each other one day by the love seat, the grand dame of the place swept into the small room, which was called a den, but the name really isn't important.

(*At this particular junction, I agree entirely with the cat, with Jane. From my own experience, I can honestly say that it is difficult for a writer to know for sure which details of a description are important and which aren't, but in this case, I believe Jane's instinct was correct. E.T.*)

She did truly sweep into whatever room she entered, for Maisie was covered with flowing, sweeping fur, creamy-colored hair that actually touched the floor, and she did half glide, half flounce along when she was stimulated to move quickly, and she held up a tail that resembled an old-style dust mop. I later began finding clumps of little hair mice by the score all over the rugs, although Maisie herself, in her plump and flowing form, would never have been caught dead with a real mouse in her mouth!

Yes, you could tell she was a special feline, a lovely mocha confection, with just the tips of her ears and bushy tail a rich chocolate color. Maisie looked like something you'd see in the Garden of Eden or some great palace in a magazine. Yes, except for one thing about her: It was that her face looked as if it had been bashed in; her nose was almost flat, had no shape at all; you could hear her dampish breathing when she fluffed into the room. Nevertheless, one could tell she was confident in being very special, very beautiful and in the fact that her glorious coat, particularly, established her as standing a cut above the rest of the world.

"Dahling ..." She made as if to rub against Danny's head; she inclined within an inch of his right ear, but in the manner of some fussy types, she cleverly missed actually touching it. "What have we here?"

I had retreated quickly myself but could see, hear, and smell just enough to know anything I wanted to know at that point, enough to know to stay behind the cloth.

"Well, this is Jane," said Danny. "She's been outside ...wandering here and there, round about ... and now ... she's ... in here ... inside. You know?"

"Oh, I know, don't I. Another little stray, at loose here on our lovely carpets. But not for long, I suppose." Maisie raised her voice to be sure I heard her. "Not here for long, I imagine." She lowered her head to look at me underneath the love seat. "What a strange little thing." She gave a hiss and pulled back out. "Scruffy. Like all the others. Well, you have to feel sorry for them, I suppose." She whispered to Danny: "They all just disappear, don't they."

"I don't know." Danny sounded worried.

"You don't remember, do you, dahling? You were such a little bitty thing. Maybe you hadn't even been brought here yet yourself." She seemed to want to remind Danny of his position below her in the house. As she sniffled along the edge of the sofa, the fur on her neck drifted backwards like some loosened scarf.

And then she swiped at me sideways under the cloth, hit my nose, and left.

I must have relaxed my guard, thinking of being strange and disappearing like the others. Still, one doesn't expect such a vehement reaction toward a kitten. I could have expected it had I been even a month older.

(Later, Jane found out why Maisie had reacted so strongly and why she had no fond place in her heart for kittens at all. E.T.)

Meanwhile, I just stepped back and tried to lick my nose. Danny offered to help, but I declined. I didn't want to hurt his feelings, but I'd begun thinking of many troubles at that point, and one of them, maybe not the biggest one, but one of them, was what might happen if dog liquid got into a cat wound. I'd no way of knowing, then, of course.

When she left the area so quickly, I figured Maisie was only mildly interested in confirming dominance in a territory she already owned and the only reason for her lack of interest must have been that what she said was true, that I wouldn't be around for long, as she said. Like the others. And thinking of that along with my unfortunate appearance brought my confidence down.

"I'm sure I heard the Mistress say you could be … here … could stay here," said Danny.

"'She spoke of another place too; I think she meant here only until I was fattened up a bit and a bit more friendly."

"You seem friendly to me all right."

"I bet Maisie wouldn't count me as a friend."

"I know what. I'll just show I'm gratefully happy whenever I see you. We'll play all the time, I'll let you crawl over me, and they'll never have the heart to take you away."

"But what about the 'others'? Were they all cats? Weren't you happy to see them, and didn't you let them crawl all over you too?"

"Well, there must have been quite a few others, but before my time. I only remember one. He was black and white, a funny little thing. He was older, though, and he was only here a little while. It's true." Danny looked worried. "But also, he didn't like me. Not at all. I was a puppy still, awfully full of puppy life, major 'activity oriented', as the Master said.

"When they brought that cat inside, he was a dirty mess, too. Oh, well, I didn't mean to- No, no, he was much worse than you— full of fleas, all bitten up, your typical tomcat. But I didn't mind all that; I didn't, no; I like dirt, and I really did want to be a buddy to him, I really did. Tried lots of games, tried to clean him up some, work with his tail, and so on. But no way. I don't know exactly what happened to him later, but he hated being inside also. You know? He was used to the roaming life, I guess. One day, when the Mistress went to take out the trash, he just left, never to return. Never returned to the indoor life, not to my knowledge, not to this house anyway. We know the Mistress puts food outside on the porch for all kinds of creatures who may need it, so maybe he's one of the lucky ones out there."

"I know there's a big tom cat who-"

"Hangs around next door?"

"That could be the one, Yep."

(Jane had obviously forgotten her attack by the black and white cat on the porch where she'd first stayed. That must have been the one Danny had tried to befriend, not the yellow one next door. There's no way to be sure, but in my research I've found no example of a black and white cat growing up to be orange. Well, I have to forgive Jane for her mistake; it's common to repress unpleasant memories. I've forgotten quite a few. Fortunately, the color of this cat has little or no impact on the story plot at this time. E.T.)

"I don't think you have to worry about him."

"No, but I do think I have to worry about disappearing the way Maisie suggested."

"My plan is going to work. I have a feeling it is. Just stay close and try to look either cheerful or forlorn or hungry."

Just about that moment, we heard the Mistress in the kitchen; we both had the same idea at the same time: We could try out our plan! Maybe we'd given a treat: Danny could sit right by the refrigerator door and look forlorn and hungry; I could sit right beside him, looking up, forlorn and hungry. So, we headed off through the living room.

We've seen some wonderful moments here in this place, Mah. I hope I can stay. I have wished over and over that my tongue could speak Human, could ask a question or two about the possibilities for my life in this house.

Well, but there's no question about my love for you, Dear Mah, wherever you are now.

Your kitten still,
Jane

Later:

In the next few hours and all my second day there, I observed the routines and activities of all the lodgers, especially Maisie. I knew to keep a constant eye out for her. As it happened, as Danny might have said before, Maisie was not what you'd call a fireball of energy. She was essentially inert; she felt no desire to exert herself, not for doorbells, nor thunder, not for sirens, nor horns. She was a study in lethargy; she used a stool to reach the armchair and, aside from our food chest in the kitchen, I never once saw her leap onto anything higher than her uplifted tail and never a counter top. Danny says this is because her foot hair, in wisps growing between the pads, makes her landings slippery, uncertain, and, therefore, unsafe; she has no firm grip on a smooth surface. As far as her lack of other activities is concerned, Danny says she just had too many demands put on her in earlier life.

And she is a poet, for another thing. Lots of times, when she is just sitting still, staring off into space, sphinx-like, in her sedentary way and without visible signs of physical or mental activity, she is composing a work of poetry. It seems that inside this richly fur covered head, vivid perceptions are churning their ways to the surface, even while, from the outside, not a ripple can be seen.

Much of her poetry that I heard and saw, it's true, had to do with resting—qualities and quantities of rest, places to rest best, that sort of thing. Here's the first one I remember:

> At five o'clock, the only fall
> Of light I find, in Winter months,
> Will lie by the Philodendron vine
> Along the steps in the front Hall.

I'd never heard a poem before that I was aware of. Were there some of them in the books the woman read to the children in our first house? I don't know if I know what they are supposed to sound like, but to me this one sounded fine; I like thinking of the light around the vine. But Danny says a lot of them are very inconsistent and pretty irregular in their "rhythms" and "rhymes". I guess those aspects could make a difference, especially if you are familiar with the broad span of poetry over the years. And of course, Danny grew up with it.

So, I tried to figure out what to expect of Maisie. Was she mainly the contemplative poetic type—or the more fiery explosive type? I expect, most likely, an unpredictable combination of both, especially, I bet, where I am concerned.

And, I expect we'll eventually find out!

Jane

BOOK I

Part Four

In which Danny reflects on his life with Jane and Maisie and then goes on with a letter of Jane's:

As Danny recalls, in their first meeting, both Jane and Maisie demonstrated some hostility; he recalls seeing Jane hiss back at Maisie from under the love seat; whereas Jane is pretty sure that she did not. In any case, Danny does know that the Mistress called Maisie away to the kitchen or there might have been a more harmful confrontation, and that he and Jane waited a long time before it was safe to go off on a tour of the house. Oh, yes, Maisie took her own long time in eating the special animal cracker treat she got for not attacking Jane.

Danny can't remember seeing the two cats in an actual roll-around fight, but he did hear dreadful noises of unwelcome greetings sometimes. The Master and Mistress would hurry around to end them. And Danny would be the first to say that there is no more fearful sound in his experience than that of two unfriendly cats expressing their thoughts at having come upon each other inconveniently—or, more likely, unexpectedly—day or night. Surely, these are the sounds of dying things, sounds we don't want to hear from a loved one. Low growls, then long-drawn-out yowls. And so Danny would also be the first to spring into action to stop

81

the unpleasantness; a fire truck rounding corners had nothing on him; his claws slashing the floor, he'd rush to locate the combatants, calling out for the humans to join him there. He would find the scene of conflict quickly, but often, by the time he arrived, all would be quiet. After a while, the Master and Mistress didn't even show up, just went back to whatever they'd been doing and left him to take care of things. Danny didn't mind that exactly, considered it one of his duties, and so on, but he did miss the company and praise of the humans. Everyone wants praise and recognition, he thinks, even for a duty.

So, at any rate, it seemed very unlikely that he was ever going to see the two cats sleeping on the same pillow together. Something kept them apart. For one thing, they both had a fixation about food and each one acted as if the other one might eat everything in both dishes, leaving nothing behind. Danny was aware that he himself would do it, would eat all the food in the dishes if he could, but he excuses himself for that because he knows perfectly well that dogs always do that. He knows, in fact, that dogs will eat even when they're not particularly hungry; he, himself, checks during regular intervals each day to see if the kitchen garbage can is open, and, if it is, he'll eat most of what's reachable even if he's just finished his regular meal. Or if he hasn't finished a meal and a human passes near the can, he'll leave in the middle of his assigned meal to check in case there's been a spill or accidental drop of human food from a human who's missed the can; he always prefers to fill up on something unusual or special and save the same old thing in the same old food bowl for later when there's nothing else.

Until Jane came inside, Maisie had been pretty casual about food, not exactly your traditional picky eater but not a second-helper either. With Jane in the house, Maisie acted like she didn't believe there'd ever be another meal in her bowl. She sat and frowned for more. The Mistress kept the cats' food dishes on a chest in the kitchen, but even jumping up and down everyday didn't seem to improve Maisie's "waistline," as they say. She got flabby and went into a slump.

Danny, of course, couldn't reach it, the cats' food, that is.

In any case, as Jane has related, Danny and Maisie had never been what you'd call close even before Jane was brought in their house. He and Maisie were not in the habit of talking back and forth together. No. But Maisie would talk on her own; maybe she talked just to herself, but sometimes, Danny thought he was supposed to be listening. She would wander through a room, her eyes half closed, and when Danny, even inadvertently, did hear what she said he learned about her early life as a show cat, how she was fed and pampered as she followed the Cat Show Circuit. This was before Danny's time. For all he knows, it could have been a figment of her imagination, something to do with being a "poet," something poets did for inspiration or such. Well, it's true that as she went on and on, eventually she'd get to the part about how poets have to lead desperate lives so as to suffer and sharpen their sensibilities, so as to learn how to write about the struggles of the world, of all the different walks of life. Overall, there were many nights, though, when Danny was specifically invited to listen to the poems, and he knew he was *supposed* to listen, when she would recite her work to him, after supper. When he wanted to take a nap.

> I've heard the sounds of life outside
> My ribbon-covered cage.
> Where I waited, silent, endless hours
> Into endless days.
> Waited to be poked, and judged,
> Waited in my cage.

(Well, this poem goes on for a while like that, so Danny and I decided to abbreviate it somewhat, to get right to the end. E.T.)

But no one sings in the judging rings.

For as long as Danny knew her, Maisie could not carry even a basic tune, never sang a note; so Danny has concluded that the line at the end of the poem about singing has something to do with a poetic license. (*Danny and I have discussed the possibility of defining the term "poetic license" or of deleting that section, but Danny feels his explanation above reveals something of his background, educational level, and personality, and that the reader may appreciate understanding these things. E.T.*) Danny finally concluded that if the singing needed some kind of license, maybe the whole poem might be restricted, but since he didn't see anything around her neck, then maybe it didn't make any difference, and he never knew for sure. Still, he liked this poem better than most of the others. He liked poems to have at least a little rhyme at the ends of their lines.

Jane, in her time, became convinced of a deep poetic truth in some of the poems, of some eccentric poetic thoughts, but then, Jane had more in common with Maisie, on a root level, than Danny ever did or wanted to.

When he'd first come into the house as a puppy, Danny had tried to become friends with everyone there, including Maisie, as he had with the black and white cat when it arrived. At that time, of course, Maisie had aged about six years, human time. But to Danny, she always acted five years older than she was; nevertheless, he made great efforts: He'd put his front legs down and pant a little in the play position called "gutup," but she'd sit there on the refrigerator, frozen as a china vase. She would look from the corner of her slightly closed eyes to a spot just above his head; it was the most dismissive look he'd ever seen on the face of an animal. Even at his early age, he felt embarrassed to be opening himself up to such a look, to be inviting an interaction for fun and have the other creature just look past him without even having the courtesy of inventing a reason for refusing, without giving some verbalized, polite excuse for declining:

*I have a headache.
*It's late.
*I have another engagement.
*I have to eat in a minute, or sleep, or wash my fur and face, ears and feet and neck and legs and tail, etc.
*You're too big and rough.

The master always explains when he can't play.

Well, Maisie turns out to be a great one for looking down on others.

Now, to go on with the next letter:

JANE LETTER #11

Dear Mahrowh,

After I toured the house as mentioned in my last letter to you, I spent two or three deceptively peaceful days before I was unexpectedly and brutally attacked by the cat Maisie. That afternoon, the woman had taken Danny out for a walk, which was unbeknownst to me when I awoke from a nap. All was quiet. I yawned, slipped from under the love seat a few inches at a time, and was just stretching out nicely when I heard a low growl, and before I could retrieve my back left leg, Maisie had flung herself down on top of it.

She must have been waiting on the seat above me the whole time I was napping below, or who knows for how long. (Did I tell you how good Maisie is at waiting. It's her main occupation as far as I can see.) But this day, when the time came, she moved as fast as a dry mop when company is at the door. She grabbed past my leg and before I could say "shrimp scampi," she was on top of me. She is so thick, so full of fur, that I could not get a claw hold or mouth hold on her, anywhere. I, in contrast, was still a skinny wreck of a thing with lots of boney protrusions, easy to find and grab.

She was trying to reach my neck, of course, but as I twisted to try for hers, it was my ear that she took in her mouth. I gave a yowl with a mighty pull, got a claw hold on the rug and managed to scrape away to safety, hair so stiff on my head and tail you'd have thought I could not fit under the edge of the little love seat. Then, by the most merciful good fortune, Maisie sat back. She was too bulky or maybe too proud to follow me. Well, it's true that I turned immediately and faced her—hissing, ears flat, claws out and ready. I seemed to know, either by instinct or your teaching, Mahrowh, that from such a position, even a small cat can inflict a big wound.

Maisie sat in front of the love seat for a long time; then, she lay down. She stayed there until Danny and the woman came back.

After such disasters as these, it is customary to speak—or write, in this case—of one's reactions, of the lessons one has learned, and of one's plans to reform in the future. So, I will say that I was thankful this attack had happened when and where it did, early in my new life and near the love seat, and I would like to point out, as is often done also, that it could have been much worse—a statement that is usually made in light of any disaster that occurs and that is, no doubt, always true too, at least for those left healthy enough afterwards to contemplate anything at all. As for the future … Well, I do plan to decide to think about some of that. The future. I don't know what power I have to decide about it, though.

I sat crouching under the love seat, the name of which is accumulating a more and more ironic connotation, and I spent the time until supper literally and figuratively licking my wounds. As the light dimmed, I napped a bit, and I awakened to see Danny's large yellow back pressed up against the love seat bottom, very nearly beside me; he must have come in to see me soon after his walk. So, I woke him up to tell him my sad story:

"She sure scared every bone in my body," said I with a little yow.

"You know, I thought I smelled the fear that comes from a recent combat operation; I smell it all around this area," said Danny.

"It was around here, all right."

"Well, she scares me, too," he went on to say.

"Maisie scares you still?" I was slow to take in this information, and I did a sort of head-scratching thing because I wondered how long a dog the size of this one could possibly be afraid of a cat the size of Maisie.

"No one tells her what to do," Danny said, "and she's a lot bigger than me, you know."

"Well, it's true you must feel, as a dog, that you have to stop doing anything the man tells you not to do, which is not to jump on Maisie, and then also you go along and do anything that he tells you he wants you to-"

"It's nothing to do with feelings or the man, Jane; it's a plain fact that-"

"I know, I know. OK, I see the obedience part, only I don't see it when the man is not in the room. But OK, I will accept that part … but Danny…" I was trying not to sound like a teacher, "it's true that when you were a puppy, Maisie looked a little bigger than you; maybe you even figured a baby would always be smaller than an old cat … when you were a puppy. Who knows? But now that you have grown up to your full size, I can tell you for sure: I can see you both, and you are fully three times higher than Maisie and about two times wider.

There was a pause.

"I am?"

"You are. Taller and fatter, uh, I mean to say, stronger."

"That much …bigger. Hmm. How much?"

"Very much—10 or 12 times as much."

"I don't think so."

"I bet that even as a puppy, you were faster and stronger, maybe even heavier and taller than Maisie because most of her size is just fuzz."

"I don't think so."

"She convinced you of her power once when you felt little, and now she has you under her control."

"Do you think so?"

"'I do."

"But Jane, how can you know that? You weren't even here. You weren't even born. She was here first. And you didn't even know any dogs yet when all that happened."

"When all what happened?"

Sometimes, Danny isn't entirely logical in his way of thought, but that's OK. Love and loyalty are more important than logic as far as I am concerned. Still, his whole misconception of size, especially his size compared with Maisie's, really bothered me.

"Back then." He tried to explain.

"When?"

"When Maisie scratched my nose, not once but twice."

"Listen, Danny, I'm just doing some calculations. I figure, we look at Maisie now, at her total grown-up size and we look at you now, at your total size, and we figure it doesn't matter how big you were then. Don't you see? You are still a lot bigger than she is *now*, from any angle."

"Not that I know of, Jane."

"You must weigh 70 pounds to her 17 now."

"I was about eight weeks, human time, back then, I think."

"Well, I haven't seen that size dog, I admit."

"My nose is my most sensitive exposed part," he said. "That's the way it is. She hit it twice. There's no going back."

No going back. He was so definite in the end. It's amazing how tenacious our early animalhood conditioning can be. I figured nothing I said would erase the pain and reverse his perception of Maisie as the older—hence, larger—one, the one with better weapons, the more important one, the one to be afraid of, the one to be in control. I could see it would be foolish of me to think of Danny as a protector, and it was just as well to know where I stood.

So, we let go of the subject for once and all.

I will let go of this letter too now. It's late in the night. But I think of protectors and I miss you the most.

> Your kitten,
> Jane

Later:

The next day, that is, today, I have found that sometimes Danny will sit or lie still when Maisie approaches us and will allow me to take refuge between his front legs, behind his front paws, or in the crook of his elbow. This knowledge came to me by chance this afternoon.

Danny was resting by the desk in the library; I was trying to climb up the door frame and had just made a third leap (That painted wood is slippery!) when Maisie surprised me there, hissed loudly, and let out one claw-filled paw. I tried to twist away and fell, head over tail, sprawling flat; then, on a run, I jumped into that spot between Danny's front legs and scrunched back as far as I could. Danny stayed quite still by the library desk; he did not move an inch. And Maisie stayed still in the middle of the doorway, her hair all puffed out as usual. Then, as we animals held our ground, Maisie didn't hear the woman when she came to the door.

"Danny, what a strong friend you are. You will shelter your kitten. You two will stick together, I see." She leaned down to rub my ear. "And you, our dear grey kitten … Look at you, holding your ground again, in a clear way, so smart and brave at once. You could be a certain Lady Jane Grey or maybe, Seymour, Lady Jane Seymour … Well, with either name, little Jane, as it turns out, we want you to stay with us. For one thing, you are so like those brave women of England who showed such daring and courage—theirs with politicians, yours with an opossum and a Persian. Other people might not ever see that side of you and might not know your strength just from looking at you. But everyone can see how Danny Lunder loves you, and the truth is, Maisie has never become a good friend to him. So, even without your strength, we can see you are a good cat for us, a special and a good cat."

The woman went to the desk and picked up some papers or mail. I went under the desk to settle my nerves and clean up my fur. I felt happy and safe. And I thought that even if I don't think of myself as such a brave cat, so long as the woman thinks I am, I gather she will let me stay in this place.

I think I will never go out of a door or under another porch again.

And, as far as thinking goes, I also think that, although he seemed not prepared to go forward in action, at least Danny Lunder seemed not inclined to go backward in retreat either. And even if the woman hadn't come along when she did, I have a feeling that Maisie wouldn't be willing to take on the two of us, Danny and me, at one time.

So, with Danny nearby, then, I feel better about my chances of finding comfort in this new house. I also assume, in light of the conversation Danny and I had yesterday, that I will be growing larger myself, every day. I must make sure to eat well, stay alert, and know where Danny Lunder is at all times. So my chances do look better today.

And isn't it lucky the mistress here knows my name, too!
Jane

BOOK I

Part Five

In which Danny reflects on his size and the letters reflect the Garden of Eden and similar archetypal settings of youth and innocence:

When Danny read Jane's last letter, he tried to remember the conversations in those first days, especially the ones about his size and strength and how he was bigger and stronger than Maisie. It seems to him that Jane went on and on about that. Looking back, he can see how unaware he was of himself and his place in the world around him at that time. Looking back, he can see how much he has learned since those old days. Now, of course, he has a much better understanding of his capabilities; he knows he has good physical strength, and he's had experiences to prove it, some good, some not so good, but as Jane used to say, "Life being what it is, you just have to learn whatever you can from whatever it is that happens."

But then, why would he think a cat was bigger and more dangerous than, for instance, a squirrel or, say, a terrier? Life is strange. He recalls an experience he had one day when he'd accidentally left the house without his leash, but that's another story ... He'd encountered a short-hair Terrier type in an alley that dead-ended up against a restaurant he was checking out. This mini-dog was sitting in front of the only garbage can whose top was partially off. The little thing couldn't have possibly reached high enough to get into the can, even if the top had been all the way off. So, Danny wagged the old tail and trotted up to see what was going on. Well, that dog set out to dancing around like a kitten in front of a Blue crab, yipping like he had a close pin on his tail. Danny slowed up. Terrier types are brazen—the smaller they are, the more so—and a dead-end alley might bring out the worst in a Terrier. Danny stopped. But a moment later that dog attacked, would not let go of Danny's left hind leg. Danny turned and reversed, this way and that, finally gained victory by taking hold of that Terrier's tiny little-

(I have explained to Danny that he has said enough to convey to the reader the truth of his superior strength and courage, at least where small dogs are concerned, and now, thanks to my timely intervention, we are free to move on.

There follows a series of letters in which Jane describes the joyful side of her early life with Danny and the man and woman, the only downside being Maisie, who was seldom joyful and never predictable. Danny will tell you that, after an unfortunate beginning, this section of the letters reveals Jane's most playful side and other personality traits that endeared her to the family in his house. And they do indeed describe that idyllic period of time we all experience early in our lives despite the Maisies of this world and before whatever major hard times and disasters may be likely to set in. E.T.)

JANE LETTER #12

Dear Mah,

I may not have written yesterday that, after the Mistress spoke of accepting me into the home, she began talking of something she called "The Vet." I remembered hearing the word somewhere, but then, before I could think of exactly where, she reached down and encircled my belly and lifted me up in the air. I was surprised at my immediate negative reaction. I am ashamed to say that I scratched her badly and I'm embarrassed to say that she dropped me down like a rat carcass

"Ouch!" She went quickly into the little downstairs toilet room; I followed; she began running water over the scratches. I could see red from beside the sink. "Someone must have picked you up and hurt you sometime in your early life. That's too bad," she said. "Now, how can I hold and comfort you, or you, me? I guess that's one pleasure we'll have to forgo, little Jane. I guess so. But we still have to get you to The Vet somehow. We'll have to work on that."

She turned off the water, went into her pocket and offered me a little treat. Good. I felt my purr rising, and I slowly wound around the sink leg to reach her leg. And she scratched my neck.

Still, for the most part, the days so far have gone along serenely, filled with numerous kitten-instigated activities, and though I keep a watchful eye on Maisie, I do sometimes tease her, too. We have to share a small box of tiny gravel for our daily eliminations, and I have to watch that she won't catch me in there, but then, sometimes, I admit, I deliberately set out to tease her when she's there; I may sneak up behind, as one cat will another, you know— and sometimes I'll even tease the humans, the man, for instance, when I grab onto his shoe laces. He only sighs in resignation. Usually.

There's one thing I like to do in the place upstairs where the water sprays out. Two curtains hang together around the spray area, and I can go in between them to watch and try to catch droplets of water and bubbles as they roll down the inside curtain. One has to be very careful here, as with so many of life's activities: One must walk or sit on a narrow, precariously curved round rim and keep her balance—keep her balance on three legs only, of course, if she is to have a batting paw free—and she must keep her mind on not striking out with that paw too vigorously or too far if she is to keep from losing balance.

One morning, early, the man stood in there with the water spray, singing "O Sole Mio" and splattering large clumps of soap suds against the inner curtain. I love to look through those colorful circles sliding down to the bottom rim! I got excited and lost my head. Instead of a single bat, I grabbed for a suds ball with both of my front paws. Well, I caught, by mistake, the man's leg along with the shower curtain between my unsheathed claws. And the man sang, "O, Sole Mi-Ouuugh!" Which I thought was very sociable of him, very friendly, to use my own language which I didn't even realize he knew as he hardly ever spoke to me, one on one.

But then, from what came next, I determined I was wrong in thinking he was being cordial. No, no. He began thrashing his body around, kicking this way and that and calling for the Mistress, something he did without fail whenever anything went wrong concerning us animals.

> (*Danny remembers times when one of the cats would throw up a stomach hair mouse in the kitchen at night, and when the Master came down in the morning, if Danny hadn't seen it first, the Master would cover it with a bowl and call for the Mistress. He would stand off in the doorway until the Mistress came down and cleaned up the mess. And, according to Danny, if no one saw it first, and the Master did step in it and hop around on one foot, all animals would disappear from the area. E.T.*)

Anyway, he must have been startled by my actions. I, in the meantime, after swaying back and forth a bit, had ended up momentarily with my two front legs on the one side of the tub rim and my two back legs on the other, and the man still turning around aimlessly, wiping his eyes, unable to see me. Then, what with all the splashing and thrashing going on, I began to slide, sinking slowly, head first, down the water side of the rim into the spray.

And he saw me then.

He picked me up in his large, dripping hands. I was too shocked to protest. He was shaking, and I felt sure that for me the end was near. But he was only doing that heaving happy thing that humans do and call it "laughing." He held me out away from his chest: "So it's you, my little trouble maker, and now you're in more trouble and feeling pretty uncomfortable too I bet." And he turned off the water with me dangling from his other hand, dripping wet by then, miserable, as he set me down outside the curtain.

Next, seeing that all this was certainly an animal problem, he called for the Mistress, who was already on her way. And they both laughed. And Danny laughed. Only Maisie did not laugh; she, not being the center of attention, left the room.

The Mistress explained how she hadn't been able to pick me up, and so on, and wondered how the man did it, and so on, and how she thought she could dry me while I stood on the floor. By that time, however, I had gathered my thoughts and was off, on my way to the love seat.

"Don't you want to get dry …? Jane?" I heard her words as I left. "Well, so be it," she said and went back to getting dressed.

Danny Lunder really loves any kind of water and, as I left the room, he was licking the man's wet and mildly hairy legs. As for Maisie, not only didn't she laugh, but she came and found me to let me know that, as she watched my water experience, bubbles of wild and dreadfully painful early-life images gushed up in her memory. And she began to tell me about her years as a show cat. She came and sat beside the love seat as I twisted my body up and down underneath it, trying to reestablish my fur patterns. (I tell you, Mah, it was very awkward moving around like that due to the lack of height in the low lying love seat.) Maisie said she preferred not to be interrupted in the telling of her history; she said she was telling it not as a gesture of friendship, but purely as information, things I should know for the future (whose future I'm not sure of, but she must have heard I wasn't going to disappear like the other cats did).

Maisie's story is one you will be interested in—a life very different from what I've ever heard tell, but it is late now and Danny is waiting beside his Master's side of the bed, waiting for me to come to sleep. I'll write more about the sleeping arrangements and, better still, about Maisie's early life (which Danny calls "Show Biz").

I have heard there is a bed filled with water to sleep in, arranged so as not to make one wet I assume, but I wonder... Anyway, let sleep surround you too, my dear Mahrowh, in a dry place, wherever you are and gently restore our love, preparing us for whatever future may be in store.

Jane

JANE LETTER #13

Dear Mah,

One would hope to have learned a lesson from such a scary experience as the splashing-water time of yesterday morning, so I am chagrined to tell you that this very morning, this very next day, this kitten was right back in there with her head between the curtains as soon as the man started the water flowing. I will say, to my credit, however, that I did not get up on the rim itself; I stayed on the floor and just worked from that angle. The man didn't appear angry about it; in fact, he smiled, and he kept tossing water and suds at me, in fun, you know, pretending to drive me away, or maybe just encouraging me to move. I remember you used to say that humans enjoyed the movements of cats.

But I promised to tell you Maisie's life story and what a story it is! First of all- Later the same day and the next day: I was beginning Maisie's life story when a disruption in our daily routine took me off course: This morning, the Mistress did not come down into the food room—I mean the "kitchen"—even as the day grew into itself. She stayed upstairs where she sleeps. Humans seem to have only one place to sleep. Anyway, the man took her food to her bed, a strange behavior also. Some of it was what we called "salt crunch," which they call "bacon." I know because she gave me several pieces. Good. Then she wanted to stroke my head or scratch behind my ears; I don't know which, but I felt more like jumping the lumps under the blanket, especially when they moved. And she laughed and didn't seem to mind even when my one front claw got caught and snagged a little hole.

"Oh, Lady Jane! That's the kind of thing will get you in so much trouble with Jack. (The man's name is Jack.) But she was laughing as she said it. "He sees you ripping up all our furniture and bedspreads with your antics. I told him you'd outgrow all that before your claws would be big enough to hurt anything. Now, look at this! What am I going to say to him?"

Humans are so funny about holes, some of which they like, as in their shirts and similar pieces of cloth, others of which they really hate as in bedspreads.

At any rate, I too stayed up there most of the day, playing lump jump or else sleeping warm between her human legs. Then, in the afternoon, she got dressed and she and the man went out the door.

So, now, I have a chance to begin the Maisie saga.

First of all, did I tell you Maisie is a poet? Well, yes, she is, and appropriately enough, she began her story with a poem:

TO JANE

I'm somebody.
You are not.
How dreary it must be
To look around yourself and see
You're one of an unknown lot.

I am not really offended by Maisie's words; art often expresses great truths, and I know what Maisie thinks about me, so, I feel, there's some truth in what she says, now. But I am still very young, and I intend to become important later.

Just a little side note: After she writes her poems, Maisie usually speaks them out for us to hear, and then she disposes of them in safe places, places where they won't be found: in trash cans, for instance, or she shreds them and eats the long thin strips in place of grass fiber, something we both miss dreadfully here in the house. She doesn't want any poems left around for the man or the Mistress to find. Danny Lunder maintains that the destruction of Maisie's poems doesn't matter one way or the other, but he has been thickly saturated with them, I think. And although I am no educated creature nor a poet, I believe all attempts at creative expression should be honored. And even though not all such projects need to be put in books or museums or on refrigerator doors, they all should be kept somewhere by someone, as records of our lives.

For that reason, sometimes, as you can see, I pull one out of the trash when Maisie has left the area. She writes very short poems, as a rule, and I say: what's the harm? Of course, I can do nothing to save the ones she has already eaten.

> (*And would she have had a larger appetite, I say, such as would have saved me from having any of her poems to type; it's been a distressful job even in the interest of accurate personal history. Jane may say, along with some others, that if a poem is short or a painting, small, its being mediocre is of much less importance than if it were grandiose. Rat food poison! As Plato meant to say: Bad art, no matter what its size, is a contamination to the human spirit; Jane is entirely too tolerant, but I let her continue. E.T.*)

Maisie is an elegant cat; there's no doubt of that. But as her story went on, and I cleaned up my not-so-elegant coat, I felt no envy of her life, not at all, for, as you will see, she suffered and experienced serious disappointments and boredom. And even though this is true of all creatures to some extent, it seems to have been even more so for her. Danny says she might have suffered from delusions of grandeur that made her think she didn't deserve to suffer at all. Unlike the rest of us.

> (*Danny says he did not say "might have suffered" but "did suffer" from these delusions. E.T.*)

Because she is so refined, Maisie speaks in a refined way, of course, and in an accent I am not familiar with but which Danny says is a cultivated cat-show dialect. As she began her story I had to listen carefully, but I think I have most of it down correctly.

She flashed her tail as she began:

"You know, dahling, even in the interest of sensationalism, I would never descend to describing my kittenhood as unhappy. No, no, no. My family-of-origin situation was not any more dysfunctional than the usual celebrity-based household—at least, not in the current public sense of the words. No, no, no. No substance abuse per se, unless eating disorders qualify; we were constantly hungry, naturally, but when we were fed, it was of the type of food you common cats can never have never imagined in your life: real chicken and livers, freshly cooked daily, that sort of thing, and enriched with essential multi-vitamins."

Maisie was wrong about me not knowing real or fresh chicken; we had found such meat quite frequently in restaurant garbage cans, but to go on:

"And no physical abuse in the current sense of that word unless you count hair pulled by grooming combs as abuse. Well, it is. Or frequent bathing with soap. Which also is. So much of what we call abuse is in the mind of the abused, wouldn't you say, dahling? But we kittens were never batted around by the more mature animals. Oh, no, no, no. It simply wasn't allowed. We were all separated, you know, at a very young age. And we never even saw the children of humans much less suffered from them."

Here it was that Maisie took a moment to bite off some of the hair between her paw pads, and I asked her how long she had been with her mother, or if they had been separated later on as we had, but she didn't remember.

"I do remember and have thought very much recently, that it was not an average upbringing, not average in any sense of the word, dahling; you can forget about the kind of Utopian early life that our friend Danny Lunder experienced, the kind of "romping in the backyard sun with mother and littermates" early life. No, no, no. We were all specially bred, you know. We were kept clean and apart from each other; we were pampered to an abnormal extent in the place where I was bred and born. So, as I say, I have concluded that dysfunction comes in many forms: I see cages in my mind. We were all in cages, you see. I see now, too many cages. Too many rules. And, well, let's be honest, dahling, too many felines—cats everywhere."

(Danny is adamant to say that he also had an above-average upbringing, that he is a pure-bred Labrador retriever, he thinks; he thinks he has some official papers somewhere, and he knows he was raised in a cage also, part way. I, myself, can't understand this thing about cages. The whole concept escapes me. Well, to continue. E.T.)

"We were fed at this and that time and exercised at this and that time and brushed and fooled with regularly at all times, all hours of the day and night, around the clock, surprise, surprise! Then put back in cages."

I couldn't help but wonder if that's how her face became so squished in, trying to get out of cages all the time. After a moment's pause she continued:

"And then there'd be days of more intense fussing over— perfumed baths, more hairdryers and combings, teeth brushings, nail clippings, all of which led up to a day that began before light with people rushing around every which way, when we'd not be fed but put in carriers. Then, in cars or vans. Then, in a vast expanse of a room and it was sit, sit, sit in cages, as usual, surrounded by more cats than usual, hundreds of cats and people brushing them. For days on end."

I began to see how it was that Maisie became so good at waiting.

"Then, at last, at last, came the moment we were there for; at least, I suppose, some of us were. This was what was called "The Judging," and this was the moment that all the fussing and preparation led up to, standing on a table, being poked all over by a stranger, and then having to look at some idiotic little feather things they used to stimulate our personalities: jiggle, jiggle … 'Look bright and smart,' they want to say. 'Ho, hum,' I say.

"In the end, if you got one of the ribbons they were handing out, everyone screamed and gave you canned salmon on a plate. And let me tell you, fresh grilled salmon? Maybe. Canned? Not worth it. My gawd.

"I don't want to say any more about that part of my life.

"And so, after what seemed like an eternity of ins and outs of carriers and cages, suddenly, one day, it stopped, just like that, and the next day, when I felt that little tingle in my tummy, I was exposed to and invaded by a male cat I'd barely spoken to before. I'd thought he was just a random acquaintance. But it became more than that. What I will say is this: there were some moments of physical gratification and even more of extreme emotional disquiet, naturally, as with any mammalian sexual experience, and then there were, my gawd, dahling, kittens. What did I know?"

(I have put my feet down and absolutely forbidden Danny Lunder to comment about feline or any other type of sexual behavior. He whines that he has something to say, but we know we do not want to hear anything about sex from a dog's perspective. E.T.)

Maisie took a moment to gaze off toward the kitchen. Her eyes clouded over, or maybe it was just the way the light reflected from her cataracts. Then, with a nostalgic sigh, she continued:

"Well, naturally, motherhood brought with it moments of untold joy. My mothering instincts came into play when I first saw the little wrigglers, each one slipping out like helpless baby birds, four of them, so wet and slimy, needing to be dried, and then the cozy, warm bundles looking so proper—all lined up, kneading away, sucking everything in sight, rumbling like little volcanoes. Unfortunately, this peaceful stage was a fleeting one. Believe me, darling, volcanoes do erupt. It was only a matter of *days* before the little buggers were crawling all over me like the hands of sixteen judges; let me tell you, in two weeks, they were poking their little transparent claws into my eyes. Needle sharp. If you think just because those claws are tiny and thin they are not painful, you may think again.

"The little suckers simply drained all my strength; their mewlings made me physically ill, and usually signaled potty calls, one after each feeding, eight or more eliminations a day that I simply refused to clean up in the traditional way; instead, I pushed everything under the bedding. That went over with my keepers like a wet hairball, dahling, as you can imagine. They looked at me as if *I* had missed the litter box. Meanwhile, the little poop makers went on pulling and chewing me 'til I was a shell of my former self. My coat dulled. I lost two pounds. I had no direction, no life of my own. You would have been looking at a typical and miserable stay-at-home mom. Let's just say, after a few weeks of that little adventure, I'd had my fill. Let us say that I chose a different path, that I moved away from those artificially imposed responsibilities, moved as far away as I could, in a birthing-cage situation.

"It wasn't very long before I ended up here." She looked around the love seat almost as if she had forgotten where "here" was. I felt strangely apart from her at that moment, and even though I wanted to ask her questions, I couldn't say a word. After a while she spoke again:

"Well, my dear, I can see now that my former life amounted to nothing more than a meaningless show, but looking back, I admit there were days I had felt flattered to be such a center of attention, looking out through the ribbons that covered my cage, listening to the astonishment of the humans at how many there were. Still, as I say, looking back and compared with life now, I can see I am much more my true self in this place, much more creative … here. I haven't thought about the kittens for a long time. Poor things. I used to picture them grown up and at the shows, in the cages, with the ribbons … plates of salmon … Now I try not to think of it. The moving finger writes, you know."

> Oh, kittens, my kittens, our pathways have diverged.
> Your mother gave you all she could
> Then she succumbed to nerves,
> Unlimited.
> And desire for a greater good!

Maisie looked at me with eyes full of—perhaps it was remorse or, perhaps, pride. I found my eyes attracted to her tail, which continued to twitch at regular intervals, and before you could say "catnip scratching post," I was on that tail and rolling it around. A moment's indiscretion, a dangerous but ultimately helpful one; when I heard her screech, I took off running; I didn't know where. I was faster. I made this important discovery: since she had lived here, maybe she had compensated for not ever having enough of all that special chicken or salmon she'd craved in her youth and, subsequently, she had laid on extra fat layers underneath her hairy coat. I found Maisie's size to be deceptive, and her speed pretty much zero.

I ended up circling around and sliding back under the love seat, which, in my fear and shock, I had totally forgotten about at first. From that safe place, I called out "sorry" sounds. In the end, as I say, I gathered a piece of confidence from this little episode. I learned that I could outmaneuver Maisie—at least, when I could see her, I could. Well, of course, that might be tricky, that condition of seeing where she is, and at all times. That will keep me on my toes. Poetically speaking.

I wish I could see you, my own clearly remembered Mahrowh and roll around with your dear tail.

> Your kitten,
> Jane

P.S. If I keep a close eye on Maisie, maybe I can learn to write poetry too.

JANE LETTER #14

Dear Mah,

As you can tell from my last letter, I continue to sort my relationships among the creatures here in this house. Danny Lunder, the dog, has been a friendly one from the first, and the Mistress as well. The man is not exactly unfriendly but just, I would say, inscrutable; the thing about him that's different from the Mistress is that he usually makes such loud sounds, loud sounds and quick movements, such things that to us cats usually point to uneasiness at the least, great danger at the most, or at the very least a kind of excitement deserving great attention, something like the time that Starling and its nest fell down the chimney in the house where I was born...What commotion! Those kinds of things shake everyone else's attention and often land one in unexpected places with a foot on one's tail. I find it hard to determine this man's notions. Except for the bath water, I just keep a dog or two lengths away most of the time. Another factor of difference is that he is heavy; his feet come down heavily wherever he moves—on the stairs or on the regular floors——and his hand falls heavily whenever he might reach out to my head, thus a pat becomes a plunk. Danny and the Mistress don't mind, and even I don't feel a true fear of him. I think he's just one of those humans who carries on a lot. (You remember, for instance, the little boy in our old house.) As for getting along with Maisie, however, even accounting for my newly discovered confidence, she remains, as they say, a clear and ever present danger, and I never know what to expect even when she's looks to be asleep.

Well, she *is* asleep much of the time—getting on in years, as she says—and when Danny takes his rests too, especially after his walks, I often play alone. One game I still like reminds me of you and our family. Remember how you used to run and jump on that thing in the water room they call a rug and you'd grab it up with you into a sort of stomach ball. That's good fun, and good exercise too, when you bunch everything together and ponter it with your hind legs. The rug has to be a certain type. Did you know that? The floors in our old home, my first home, were mostly rug, I see, looking back. Here, there are small and large rugs placed near each other on a slippery floor. I must ask Danny what this floor is made of. Anyhow, some rugs I've found are very stiff and thick, and although these are fine for claw stretching, they don't roll up very nicely. Well, this house is full of both kinds. I make the rounds. Sometimes, the man steps on things I've placed under a rug and says words like the man in our house together said. What these particular sounds indicate is clear anger, in general, but they don't seem to have any actual meaning, so I won't give the specific words of them at this time.

When Maisie is awake, I have to remain alert. Sometimes, she attacks very seriously, anxious to keep her dominant status intact. Other times, she actually seems to be trying to relax and play... in her old-fashioned, fancy-up-bringing, and out-of-practice way. She'll make a wild dash toward me; then, at about the halfway point, she'll stop and walk to the side, sit and lick her left front paw a little. It's as if she doesn't care to reveal why she took on that way, but since I'm never quite sure what's going to happen, I'm ready to head for the love seat on a moment's notice.

Just the day before yesterday ... I remember the scene particularly ... Maisie had been lying for hours in that semi-awake state we call "mini-dormus"—crouching, staring vaguely ahead, eyes half open or eyes closed, pretending not to be aware of the world and letting her meanness build up. Because I'm a kitten, you and all felines know that I find it hard just to crouch the same way for hours on end, but I believe Maisie's ability to do this helps balance out her position in the ongoing stalking situation between us: I am faster, but she is patient. I get bored, lose my concentration, let down my guard and, zam, there she is—like lightening before the thunder!

At any rate, on this particular day and for the above reason, I take the initiative slowly, and I approach from behind. (We don't consider a rear approach cowardly, do we? I never thought so. Well,

I hadn't ever thought about it at all until recently. When I do think of it, I think it must be a normal feline hunting strategy. I mean, it's one thing if you're in a great, large pack of predators—dogs or wolves, or such, as I've heard Danny describe; in those cases you have no crucial need for silence or stealth; you can raise a ruckus for miles around, alarm everyone within hearing distance, turn your prey into a terrified statue, stunned with uncertainty, or frighten it into a confusion of flight, this way and that, until your group finally surrounds it completely—front, back, and center. But we solitary hunters have to use another approach, and I resent the implication by some, like the man here, for instance, that our methods are underhanded and sneaky. I guess when there's any little doubt in my mind about the correctness of my behavior, I go on and on trying to explain it, a fact that, I fear, only goes to show how much I don't understand about it. At any rate, from behind was my main approach to Maisie and especially on this day.)

(*Danny recalls that he and Jane talked for hours about the food gathering methods of carnivores, and they came to agree that since there must be hundreds of ways to kill things, there's probably no one best way, so they were left to say "to each his own." As a roach, I am here to say: they should finish off with the killing, then evolve to eat anything available. E.T.*)

So, on this day, as I remember well, my plan turns and falls apart on me. I had just finished that first snack of the day, the one they call breakfast; I am sitting under a chair, feeling relaxed. Maisie is licking the rim of her bowl; she finishes and then moves slowly to her usual spot in front of the refrigerator door; she begins to clean up. (I think she finds comfort in being near the refrigerator; I think she feels hopeful that the Mistress will remember something that needs to be put out in our food bowls, something delicious that has been forgotten and is lying inside the cold door.) I move from under the Mistress's chair to under the man's chair. I sit a moment and yawn. I think I will deal with my coat later. Maisie is very busy with hers—tail swishing leisurely as she works. (I think I've mentioned how long and thick her hair is; she works, off and on, for short stretches of time all day to keep it organized. I think that's because the extended exertion would be too much for her. Licking her coat is the one thing Maisie does with total vigor. She fairly swipes away at it. I joke that she may wipe all the color off!)

But because she doesn't groom very long at one sitting, on this occasion, I need to make my way quickly but unobtrusively to the other side of the refrigerator, just around the corner from her. I want to catch her unawares, to be within reach of her tail and also within reach of an escape route. Once in place, I can see only her tail as it hangs out to the side, gently swaying. So, I find my position; I settle in crouching; I activate our little get-ready, rear end dance, the pelpalate runting one. Then … then … then, I take a leap, and at that very same moment, the Mistress opens the refrigerator door. And everything goes crazy: To avoid the door, I turn accidentally into Maisie who squeals in anger and turns onto me; meanwhile, the Mistress drops a milk bottle just as the man and Danny come back in from Danny's walk; the milk bottle splatters all over the floor, and Maisie and I take off in a flash for other parts.

All I can hear from the kitchen is jumbled loud talking, a sort of frantic high-pitched commotion. Then, the house grows very quiet; the door to the outside is opened and closed, and the house grows even more quiet. We are alone, Maisie and I, and of no comfort to each other. I sit under the love seat and wait, again, I wait. I remember to carefully watch out for Maisie, and sure enough, in a moment, I see her fuzzy paws as she pads back and forth along the front edge of my den.

"Dahling, you have really cooked your goose this time."

I am not familiar with that expression and think to myself, "Well, why shouldn't I? It's likely better that way." But I knew from her tone of voice that Maisie was full of scorn and derision and that whatever the expression meant, it was not anything so pleasant as a meal of cooked goose!

"All that fuss and confusion in the kitchen. No one likes it. And something is wrong. I can tell you that, my dear."

"What?"

"Something is wrong. Not clear on what, but I can tell you this, dahling: they left the house, all three of them together, and as far as I'm concerned, they never leave the house like that unless something is wrong."

I grow quiet; as quiet as the whole house is, I am too.

"And they know who caused it, whatever is wrong; they know you caused it. Little La tee da lady, little fancy Jane "Lady." I can tell you, Dahling, confusion like that never went on in this house when I was the only cat here, never."

"But you were in the kitchen, too ..." I sound like our little girl Jane when she wanted to put blame on her brother.

"Yes indeed, and they've known for years what a peace-loving creature I am by nature. Seldom lift a paw in anger. Very non-confrontational." She sighs. "Maybe now I'll find some of my own peace again."

Maisie takes her time exiting the room. "Farewell to you, little usurper."

I feel more alone than I did under the bushes that first night. You and Boots... our old house... out of reach. And I'm here, where I look down at this paper, the cold marks, separate from each other, like us, so far, far apart now.

Your lost kitten, Jane

JANE LETTER #15

Dear Mahrowh,

I continued to feel upset yesterday, although I managed to take a short nap and order my fur before I heard people and Danny return through the back door. Danny came at once to find me under the love seat; he looked pretty much the same, but he had a strange odor about him; I didn't like it, and I didn't come out of hiding at first. Danny said later that I even hissed at him, but I don't remember doing that.

> (*Danny is entirely sure that the hissing he remembers is correct, and although I've known him less than a year, I've never seen him so vehement about any of his opinions before. He even claims to have been frightened when it happened. E.T.*)

When he started making those coaxing snuffling noises, the ones he uses a lot when he can't reach me, I could tell he was nervous and uncertain, pleading, in his own unique way, for me to give in. He wanted me to bump and rub against his nose.

"Ith I smell thunny, iths becauseth I vint to The Vet," he said, noticing my hesitation.

Vet. The Vet. Where had I heard that word before? Oh, Mah, I do remember. I do! My little brother! That's where he went when he was crying so hard, when the children dropped him. The Vet.

"But you came back," I said, astonished at this fact.

"Hutt ou you ean? 'Course I came ack."

He showed me his tongue, all swollen along the left side. "I can ardly alk," he said, and I had noticed his words did sound full and heavy coming out.

"I ad a hot," he went on, but now I didn't know what he meant anyway.

"What's a hot?" I said. I was becoming somewhat used to the unpleasant odor coming from his fur, so I came part way out from under my love seat.

"Sot, a sot…," he said much louder.

"Let me see," I suggested, coming the rest of the way out, thinking or hoping that seeing is the beginning of getting to the reality of a thing.

"An't see it,' he said. "ack ere." He indicated his rear end.

I thought maybe he meant *he* couldn't see it from the way his head was attached, so I looked all around; I even climbed up there but saw nothing.

"I don't see anything up here."

"Can't SEE it!" He spoke even louder and sounded irritated. "Eel it."

"Oh." I began to feel around all over his butt. The vet scent was stronger back there, but nothing else was evident. I kept pressing around.

"Ot ouw. Eore. At ee vet."

I didn't know anything he meant about this whole vet discussion.

"OUGWA!" He must have felt something then.

I stopped moving and slid down his flank pretty fast. Danny put his head between his paws and cried a little, and I could tell he wasn't his old self. He was feeling bad. I could tell.

And I felt bad. I felt like I didn't want to tell him what I had done and how it was all my fault.

Later:

I found out that, in the kitchen confusion after my pounce on Maisie's tail and before anyone had noticed him, Danny had lapped up a goodly amount of the spilt milk and glass; he had cut his tongue all along the left side.

At supper, he didn't eat but five or six bites. He said it hurt when he ate the hard dog food, and he was going into a fast. The fast lasted 37 minutes. Then, the Mistress opened the cabinet and brought out a can, larger than the ones she has for us cats. Danny ate this food slowly. He explained later that, although he does like this canned food better than the dry, still he really prefers what he calls table scraps, what I call garbage. I've seen him even nose around in coffee grounds, licking up particles here and there. I think all my experience in the alleys and cans outside had a negative effect on my taste buds. To me, everything in the garbage can ends up smelling like coffee grounds, so instead of helping me cultivate a taste for varied and exotic foods, my experiences made me end up preferring regular cat food most of the time. Danny really wanted some of the sausage-like meat the man and Mistress had eaten for supper. I could tell. He said his tongue was hurting more and more.

I felt very confused being with Danny, trying to talk to him, when I hadn't told him about my part in the disaster. I'd never considered before how uncomfortable it might be to look at someone you are hiding things from. I decided to confess what I'd done, to take the risk of anger and desertion. But when to do it? There's no good time to schedule a torture like that. The sooner, the better—so I've heard. It could be true.

After a while, I went to find Danny where he was sleeping on his pillow bed; he spent time after supper with the man in the library, that same room downstairs where all the noise and movement, lights and flickerings, come from the box of television, the room where Maisie had discovered I could count on Danny's protection. Tonight, the place was quiet except for a few sad little whimperings Danny made on his out breaths. The man was in there with the book in his hands.

Normally, I'd have been curled up between Danny's front legs or else, if he were on his side, right behind his front elbows. I think I said this before. My favorite places. Well, I wasn't in them, of course. Instead, I tried a little head bump on his chin and mouth. I forgot his tongue injury and when he made a small yelp, I knew I'd hurt him. I did the wrong thing. And let me just say again: I think this happens when you are nervous and worried, and now, I see, especially when, no matter how unintentionally, you are directly guilty of hurting someone you would never...

> (*Let me just say: I have very little sympathy for nerves or worries of these kinds, and frankly I am not even sure what "guilt" consists of, though I have looked it up in several dictionaries. It must be an inherited fault of mammals. Water bugs don't encounter these sorts of incapacities. E.T.*)

... never want to hurt. Danny looked at me with his eyes half closed. He sighed when I told him what I'd done. He shook his head as if he could get rid of the pain that way. Then, very unexpectedly from my position, he gave me one terrible big and long swash with his very wounded, aching tongue. Just that, and I knew I was forgiven. And I took my place next to his body once again.

Think how much that gesture must have hurt my good friend Danny. Think how lucky I am to have such a friend!

To have such a dear and careful mother too. And so, good night from,

Your doubly lucky kitten,
Jane

BOOK I

Part Six

In which, among other things, Danny explains about the vet and ends with a terrible poem:

Danny feels that Jane is right about one thing, which is that any trip to the vet is one too many—especially when that trip accomplishes nothing, nothing Danny can tell anyway. And more especially, when the vet laughs.

But Jane is wrong about the location of his tongue wound, which was on the right side, not the left, and it was not all along his tongue but only a cut in one place near the front. It bled a lot at first, but the vet said that was good for cleaning out the wound. He said there was no need to do anything because there was no way to bandage it. He said this, and that is when he laughed. He said Danny's tongue would keep itself as clean as Danny did. And he laughed again. Of course, anyone would have known those things. No one would have known why he laughed. Then, somewhat unexpectedly, after saying all that about not doing anything, he gave Danny a shot. Danny knew a shot is usually the last step, so he just closed his eyes and prepared to leave in a hurry.

(Obviously, the man laughed when he pictured trying to affix a bandage to a dog's tongue, and he laughed again when he

Danny acknowledged that it was useless to say anything further to Jane about the vet. From what he could tell she'd never seen one and certainly had never been given a shot either. He decided that for Jane he would treat it as one of those "what you don't know won't hurt you" kind of things. But then there's no way to know which bad things must happen to prevent which other bad things from happening. Or, which would be worse.

Danny does not blame Jane alone for all those kitchen happenings and never did. That night, when they first spoke about it, however, he was getting too tired and his tongue was too worn out with eating and talking to explain that to her. "Cuff." He doesn't remember now if he ever did tell her he didn't blame her, at least not all the way. It was just as much Maisie's fault for not watching her tail and the Mistress's too for being so quick to be scared and drop a bottle.

Danny thinks carefully to himself now that if he is ever lucky enough to see Jane again, he will tell her all of the things he never thought to tell her when she was there with him. He thinks of a poem that's in his head; he doesn't remember if Maisie wrote it or not, but she must have because he is not a poet himself:

> We wander lonely as a skunk
> Across the hills of this dark plain.
> Both high and low our hearts have sunk
> To know both health and pain.

(I spoke with Danny in an effort to convince him not to include this poem, even with an apology. It is full of fallacies that, although they may be poetic fallacies, as the expression goes, are bothersome. And the skunk is not a poetic animal; the word itself is entirely unpoetical, even if what it refers to isn't, but,

of course, it is. And if there were several animals, as in "we," the word would have to be "skunks," which is even worse and would throw off the entire rhyme scheme. The "hills on the plain" concern me along with the "hearts sinking both high and low." Are these possible, and if so, are we really prepared for this kind of surrealistic imagery? E.T.)

JANE LETTER #16

Dear Mahrowh,

After spending most of the last few days upstairs in bed, the Mistress came down today for breakfast, and then the man took her away through the other door, not the porch door. As she left, she bent over to give me a nice ear rub and scratch, but I felt uneasy to see her go that way. I don't know why; the man leaves by that door almost every day, and he comes back in that way too—many days, loaded down with brown bags, some holding cat food, in fact, and others, I assume, holding human food or other things humans need. Why did I feel uneasy? Have we cats always liked bags?

On a brighter side, this morning, Danny said he felt much better. It's been 10 days now since the refrigerator incident, and this is the first time I've seen Danny show his old interest in food and the other assorted items that have fallen on the floor. I think I told you about the coffee grounds. Did I tell you about the paper towels? Some of these things make me nervous. I've seen him hold his paw on the dry edge of a used paper towel, steady the whole thing so it won't move, then lick at the wet juicy food spot in the center until everything, juice and paper, comes up into his mouth. He's happy. He swallows all the wet parts and licks his lips.

Just at this moment, I have stopped to think how funny it is that only a few weeks ago, I would never have noticed or spent any time considering how a dog felt or ate. So it is that our lives and thoughts do change. I must have been living here in relative comfort for about a year now cat time. There have been intervals in which I might have preferred another place, but everyone must feel that way at times, no matter what place she's in. At times. Bad times they would be.

My thought is that some times are mixed up as to the good and bad, so you have to be careful what to think of them. The Mistress says she can always tell if we've had fun in the night by the extent to which the soft rugs downstairs are lying rumpled about, out of place, in the morning. She thinks messed up rugs mean frolic and games; she probably thinks that Maisie and I are cozy friends by now, romping around in good-natured feline spirits from dusk to dawn. Well, yes and no.

One night, I created a rug tunnel in the water room upstairs. I crawled inside and crouched with my head almost outside the rim at one end and my tail …I'm not sure what my tail was doing actually. I could hear voices and movements in the hallway and on the stairs. I planned to wait in the tunnel and see what might happen. The world is full of half-planned, half-chanced adventures, of course; Maisie or Danny might show up, or the man might come in and be surprised.

I am getting better at waiting. I hope that doesn't mean I am getting more like Maisie. Well, right at the minute I was thinking of the devil, there she was. I couldn't see her but I knew. She must have been at my tail end. Ah. What did I expect? And she was prepared to wait and wait and wait. By that point though, I, myself, was finished with waiting. But just when I was about to make a run for it, I saw Maisie's paw at the rim of the rug, at the tip of my nose, at the head end of the tunnel after all. In that case, if I sprang out of the rug tunnel, I'd end up like a toad in Maisie's waiting face and claws! But then, neither did I like the idea of backing out in reverse because you know how irritating it is to feel your fur being ruffed up the wrong way.

I decided to creep slowly, slowly to the door; I decided the rug could come along on top of me. I would travel incognito; then, when I arrived at the door frame, I could slip out, head first, into the spacious hallway, where there are more directions in which to run for an escape. I began a slow, wavering move toward the door. From my position, I couldn't see what sort of effect the creeping rug was having on Maisie or whether she was moving along with it or not, whether she had even noticed it going away. For all I knew, she had jumped to sit on the toilet seat, where she always looks regal. Or maybe she had dozed off while leaning against the white tub, which shows off her rich chocolate hues.

So, I crept along—one, two, three steps—and then, wham! One of my paws must have slipped out in front, and Maisie was on top of the rug and me. She grabbed us with all four paws, the whole of us, one great lump together. We tumbled around in one of those furry and confusing entanglements until I slipped out from under everything and took off for safer parts.

I only wish I could have seen her face when she discovered I was gone and that her paws held only a slightly damp, very cold bathroom carpet. " Ahrawh!"

These rug games remind me of you, Mahrowh, over and over, but my thoughts are coming in slow as a creeping rug now and I'm thinking of the Mistress's warm head and neck. Good night, my first playmate. I'll write again soon, soon.

With love,

Jane

JANE LETTER #17

Dear Mahrouwh,

I am thinking still of ongoing events as well as a strange and special thing that happened this morning. I had been playing "jump the leg lumps," which turned into "bite the legs and toes" on the Mistress's bed. At some point, I even went into a rug roll type thing, bringing my hind legs into action quite wildly, pontering away. The Mistress was laughing mostly and then saying, "Oh, no!" And then trying to keep very still, and then trying to hold me very still, stroking my chin and neck. At first, I did pretend biting and licking her hands, but in a little while, I became very sleepy and my purr arose.

The Mistress talked to me on and on, and her voice is soothing. She called me all the old silly names she has—Goober Bean, Lurder, Scooper Duper, Wooskie Boober—things like that, and the water poured out of her eyes.

"I'm so glad you came here to live, Jane Seymour. I've learned some things I needed to know from you—about love, for one thing, and about how unpredictable it can be, maybe even unwanted, often unintended, and how one can accept it anyway. When you came to the porch, no one wanted to love you.

"You were surely not a beauty, in your messy gray coat all splashed with irregular creamy cloud masses, your seemingly ordinary big, green eyes. There you were.

"Then, do you remember? How you stood off the opossum that was trying to eat your food? How we knew then you were a special little thing? How you purred and let us pet you? How beautiful you became?

"A tiny body in front of a opossum on our porch. There you were. Without a reason. Then, we loved you. Our love for you seemed

123

unreasonable, too; there was your bravery, of course, but surely not just that. There was nothing to do but allow it, even follow it. Now, let me tell you, that kind of love will take one off in all directions, to the tops and to the bottoms, to sweetness because it's there, to fear of losing it, and finally to thankfulness beyond all that.

"Who could expect such a gift to wander in without a reason? I have always worked around reasons and logic: do this to gain that or be that to reach such and such, but you... just...happened..."

She continued to talk about gifts and why there should not have to be reasons for things; why outcomes didn't need to be predictable, and why they were more fun if they weren't. She talked about endings and how they could be accepted too. I slowly drifted off to sleep.

Now it is later:

The Mistress is very quiet, still asleep. I am thinking about my fur: What other creatures have said about it, what you, my mother, always said: Beauty doesn't begin or end at the fur. When I looked in the rain puddle, I must have seen only what I wanted to see. What is the truth, I wonder, about how I look and how is it important to me? And what has it to do with love? Well, I don't want to seem to avoid these critical questions, but for now I think I'll go back to sleep.

Now it is even later still, the next day, in fact: The man has started giving us the morning snack, and usually, it's all right. Sometimes, he forgets the canned food, the best part, but then if we fuss around the refrigerator long enough, he'll remember. So, it's morning, and all three of us are in the kitchen enjoying the pleasant after-a-meal heaviness, and I tell them about beauty and love and what the Mistress said last night. Danny tells me that the man once told him that beauty is in the eye of the beholder and it's only skin deep anyway—which leaves the fur unaccounted for, again. Danny says the man says very little about love, but one time, Danny heard him say to the Mistress: "If I didn't like the dog, would I take such care to fix his food and let him take me for his walks on time?" And the Mistress said, yes, he would because he has a highly developed sense of duty instilled in him by his mother.

"You blame my mother for everything," the man had said and scruffed her hair.

"Not everything," the Mistress said and gave him a little lick on the mouth.

> (*We of my genus and species have evolved far beyond the concepts of beauty and love considered here. Because we have all reached the same level in both, this whole discussion has very little meaning for us. I don't even understand it. I look and feel the same as everyone else of my kind that I meet. E.T.*)

BOOK I

Part Seven

More mulling over the topics of beauty and love, a contemplation happily followed by the description of a joyful occasion:

Looking back, Danny can see that Jane was overly concerned about the mixture of colors in her fur and how that might affect others' perceptions of her. The fact that she mentions it so often could mean something serious—in Danny's view, could mean she was uneasy about her appearance—and now, again, Danny wishes he had talked to her more seriously on this topic. For Danny loves her fur. The colors of it don't matter at all to him. He likes the soft, short length and the scent of it. Maisie's long hair messed up his nose, tickled it, and made him snort.

So much for a start at love. As for beauty, well, Danny likes the saying about beauty being only skin deep which he feels is the beauty of scent; he certainly loved being able to find Jane's skin down below her fur and breathe in the beauty of its odor, and he supposes that is what the saying means.

And as far as sleeping on the Mistress's bed and near her hair are concerned, Danny wishes to add that he would have liked to sleep all night on the humans' bed, too, like the cats, but he only did it early, before the Master got in there. The Master told him he was too big, took up too much room, but then Danny himself had a problem too: He couldn't seem to get used to the unexpected human leg movements. They made him jump up and then turn around and around to get his spot adjusted again, something that can be complicated to do. So, the Mistress had bought him a large, soft pad and put it beside the bed.

What Jane doesn't say, according to Danny, is that the Mistress had started going to sleep earlier and earlier, and what Danny will say now is that, going by her scent, the Mistress had not been her regular self in those days, and sometimes, Danny was out for his evening walk when she and Jane got into bed. Then, Jane would be lying down next to the Mistress's neck and head, but later, when Danny came back and went to his cushion, Jane would often leave the bed and come down to curl up between his legs for the main part of the night. Those were nights when Jane wasn't playing around as described previously, nights when Danny was his happiest.

(As for me, I can't imagine sleeping next to a dog, a person, or any other insect. E.T.)

JANE LETTER #18

Dear, Dear Mahrowh,

What an adventure occurred! Today, when I came down from afternoon nap and toe pouncing with the Mistress, the outside had come in. I could smell it before I saw it. I stopped short, then continued at a modified creep. I felt half fearful of the scents, scents like those I'd smelled under so many bushes beside so many porches out there in those fearful days and nights when I was without a home, and also like those that still drift in from an occasional open door at Danny's walk times. Then, there it was, in the large front room. What was it!? I'm forgetting the things I saw before … For a minute, I can't remember …

Later: I found Danny watching at the door that leads to the dark places up some stairs that the humans hardly ever use and that they try to keep us away from but that I followed Maisie up one day. Well, that's another story, but I did smell wonderful odors up there before we got caught and brought back down. Maisie said one of the odors was mice; then, she tossed her head and said they'd be covered with dust. Anyway, Danny was sitting in front of this door, making those small whining noises he does when he's excited but doesn't want to get yelled at for barking.

"What's in the living room?" I asked.

"It's called a Christmas tree," he said between whimpers and without taking his eyes from the door.

"Why?"

"I don't know."

"Um," I said. "Christmas tree. Is it different from other trees, the ones outside, like the ones you told me about with all the scents around the bottom, the ones where you-"

"It's different. For one thing, you do not pee on it. No way."

"Oh," I said.

"And for another thing, it's going to get all dry and scratchy and die, and they'll take it away. Like that."

"Why?"

"I don't know."

"Well, why are you in such a bad mood about it?"

"I don't see myself in a bad mood about it."

"I see you in one."

"Never mind, then," he said and licked up a little drool that had escaped his lips.

"I hate it when you get in a bad mood."

"I'm not."

I waited a minute or so before I wiped my cheek on his shoulder. "Does it have something to do with the dark place then?"

"Attic."

"Attic then."

"Does what?"

"Your bad mood?"

"Forget the bad mood."

"Why don't you then?"

"How'd you like it if they brought in a large sandbox, set it up right in the middle of the living room and then told you you're not allowed to use it properly ... or at all?"

"I see what you mean. Well. I'd use it anyway. I cover everything up. They'd never know."

Danny looked at me as if I were very, very small, smaller than the kitten I'd once recently been. "I don't want to talk about it anymore. I'm just going to stay in a bad mood for a while, if you don't mind, and even if you-" At that moment, the dark attic door opened and the man's head appeared on top of a pile of boxes.

"Move away, Dan ... Jane! Move! Danny! Jane!"

His voice sounded desperate, and Danny and I did move; we moved quickly to the right, and the man stepped quickly down a step at the same time; he stepped quickly to the left, although naturally, that turned out to be our right, and then the boxes came down as his foot came down beside me and on Danny's foot. And he expressed himself with words that shouldn't, Danny always says, be said in front of Maisie and me.

I think it's good of Danny to be concerned about what words Maisie and I are exposed to, so I have never told him about the man and woman in our old house and words they used all the time, not to mention the things they did like leaving two perfectly good kittens out in other people's yards. Sorry. I just got in a bad mood too by thinking back. But to go on with the boxes:

When we cats are in terror, as you well know, Mah, and I've said before, our instinct is to go up. And so, in no time flat, I climbed to a high place which was on the man's shoulders and head, where it's hard to hold on at first. After yelping once, Danny stepped back and sat down. He barked three times. I was trying to hold on to anything my feet contacted, and the man was trying to hold on to me and some of the boxes still, or maybe, he was trying to release me and put the boxes down, as he slowly lowered himself to sit on the last attic step. At about that time, the Mistress stepped into the hallway.

"Jack! What's happening? Oh. Oh, dear. I see what it was."

"Watch out." The man's voice was very low, almost sad sounding. "Don't trip over the balls."

It was then that I noticed the large number of shiny, round toys on the floor. All over the place, they were.

"Look now. There are hardly any broken ones," said the Mistress. "We'll have them gathered up in a jiffy."

I love the way the Mistress says "in a jiffy" this or that. "I'll be ready to fix your dinner 'in a jiffy'," she'll say or "I'll be over to give you a head rub 'in a jiffy'." At first, I thought it meant some kind of container she rode in.

"Here, let me see about Jane." She lifted me up, and, I couldn't help it, I began to panic. She put me down. "Well, that must have scared you too, little Seymour, no matter how brave you might be. Now, scoot away, go on, both of you."

"I could have broken my neck," said the man, "or any number of things."

"Should I check you out, then?" The Mistress took his head in both hands.

"Later."

"It's times like these we must just think to ourselves how dull our lives would be without this sort of creature excitement."

"Right. Let's do think of that, to ourselves," he said, and he began to collect the toys.

Meanwhile, Danny and I wanted to help clean up. Danny's teeth surrounded a small stuffed figure of a man with white hair all over his face. Danny chewed this thing gently for a moment to see if it was all right, to be sure it was not broken, and so on. I touched one of the shiny balls, lightly. It seemed okay to me. I tried it a little more. It was fine. I knocked it across the hall and down the stairs, and I followed, but not quickly enough to catch it, and by the time I reach the bottom, it had broken up everywhere. I touched one of its pieces. Well, so much for attic balls. Who makes these things, anyway, these kinds of balls that fall apart after going down a few stairs? I headed on back up; maybe the one I had was defective. I'd take a minute to see if a different one would be better.

But now the balls were all together and being put back in the boxes, each in its own nest—useless, I thought, but still, it was nice to see so many of them all at once.

Speaking of all at once, just about then Maisie appeared from wherever it was she had been.

"Let me guess, dahling." She spoke to Danny alone. "There's a tree downstairs in the main room."

"It's that time of year," said Danny.

"Ho hum", said Maisie.

After supper, Danny told me how Maisie acts as if she's bored by the Christmas tree but how she still allows herself to knock off as many ornaments as she can every night, especially between the hours of one and eight a.m.

"What is this knocking off of ornaments? What are ornaments? Where are they to be found?" I'm not following this conversation at all.

"On the tree," he said, and he gave me a little nudge that, at first, I thought was a result of his bad mood, but then, I got a long lick and his voice softened. "I forget you never saw any of these things. Well, I can't wait for you to see the way they hang those balls on the tree, and the way the balls shine and sparkle. But first, you're gonna see how the humans get the tree to stand up without its bottom. It takes a long time because there's no dirt in the main room, and then you'll see how they wrap twinkling lights all over the tree, top to bottom, and space them out while one of them says, 'Something needs to fill in over here.'

"You're gonna be amazed," he says.

Well, Danny was right about everything; these last two days have been sparkling. With lights and ornaments, with all sorts of new things! Lots of boxes for one, but you can't get in them; they're all to stay closed up. Did you ever see this time of year, Mah, maybe before I was born? Anyway, we've batted around whatever we could reach by now. So goodnight from a tired but sparkling kitten,

Jane

JANE LETTER #19

Dear Mah,

After it was all over, I realized that the few weeks time of Christmas contained all the kinds of things life always contains but just condensed; this was much like my life at this house in the beginning, full of everything. Some times were expected and good; some were expected and not good; some were unexpected and either one. And some were both at the same time.

For one thing, as time went on, many of the Christmas tree balls we played with every night broke, and new ones had to be found. New ones didn't bother us; we had fun playing with anything we could knock down, of course, but the man didn't like it. He grumbled because he had to go back up into the attic, bring down the boxes and, as he reminded us, be reminded of how Danny and I had almost "broken his back." And then the balls he wanted in the attic ran out. You see, at first, the Mistress said all the balls should be just silver and blue, and pretty soon, the man had to go out the side door and bring back the correct ones, in a bag. Then, it was strange; after a while the Mistress just started putting any and all the colors on together and laughing and saying it was more like life that way. So, you can see what I mean about Christmas and life.

As more days passed, another situation developed that may have been expected by someone but not me: I noticed that, in the mornings, when the lights were turned on, there were never any balls or toys hanging from the bottom to midway up the tree. Every night, between the three of us, we managed to clear off everything except, symbolically, one little figurine and two blue balls in the very back. Now, we knew both the Mistress and the man wanted all of those things to be on the tree, and we really tried not to interfere; especially during the day, we tried hard to stay away from the tree altogether.

But we failed. And we felt bad when one morning came that the two of them finally stopped putting back what we had knocked off. Soon, they only put some of the things back, once in a while, when other humans, strange ones, came into the house. Not often.

Along with the tree toys and their games, Christmas offered up other novelties, mostly unexpected by me but expected by Danny and Maisie—new odors and foods and, finally, and especially, the one day when the boxes with their papers crackled open, and their insides spilled out over the rugs. Then, without notice, I fell into a frenzy of attack, leaping from one into another pile of surprises. Strings called "ribbons" flew around with everything else; Danny and I chased them down and chewed at their ends. I'd never seen so much movement and rustle.

Even the man was laughing and throwing paper up and down; he would wind up my new pretend "Santa" mouse and cover it with layers of tissue as it wobbled along; he'd hide the string ribbons inside some empty boxes. I could get grips on the rug, which enabled me to leap especially high and crash especially hard into everything; I went here, there, and everywhere without a pause. These actions reminded me of those times I'd had with dry leaves under the bushes and around the various porches when I lived outside. Even those times don't seem so bad now, as I look back from a safe place.

The Mistress laughed until the man had to hold her up and take her to sit on the sofa. And next, he gave her things to drink and the little "pills that made her feel better."

The pills are an unexpected part of Christmas, and Danny is wary of them; he says they give off an odor he doesn't like, an odor of something just like the vet, and for that reason he expects no good to come of them. Not ever having smelled anything that I know of like the Vet, except on Danny, I can't say yes or no about the pills. I have learned to expect some things, bad or good, from some odors, and some events also; in fact, I am thinking right now, as I write this, that for something to be expected or unexpected, one has to have lived long enough to know what sorts of things do tend to happen in the world, or more exactly, tend to happen as a result of other things happening.

I now know, for instance, that if I am dropped outside, far away from the house where I was born, I will expect to find all kinds of discomfort. And, if I were left outside again and a large bowl of food appeared beside someone with a kind hand, I would know that this was a type of totally unexpected good fortune.

But sleep is coming upon me and this topic takes me too deep for such a late hour. I'm going upstairs, where I expect to find the Mistress, warm and sweet-smelling in her bed, and where she will welcome me with soft words and nudging and I'll curl up by her head.

With an expected tall yawn, I remain,

Your own kitten,

Jane

BOOK I

Part Eight

In which Danny confronts a wheelchair and the letters show how things begin to roll downhill from that point:

The day the wheel chair was brought into the house is a day that Danny remembers very well because he made a fool of himself with barking. Normally, he will bark, of course, when someone, anyone, comes around the house, about within 25 feet or so, but usually, he can identify the scent and shut down the alarm inside himself within a minute or two as the scent bearer gets closer.

On the day in question, he'd never smelled anything like the combination of odors he was getting from the yard. One was that of an unknown human (he could tell that much); one was some kind of metal for movement, like a car or such; and one he couldn't identify at all at first. He caught the scent of something recently familiar, and he was even more alarmed than he had been! The nurse! The pills! It was like all of those! It was something vaguely resembling, The Vet, the scent of the vet house …or something like that; there it was again, just like the nurse! His bark took on a slightly higher pitch and a frantic, more rapid beat, and the sounds would not let up.

Now, as it happened, this wheelchair incident occurred some short time after this new kind of mistress, called "the Nurse," began to stay in the house during most of the day. So, it was she who finally came down to answer the door that day. She was not happy to see Danny waiting there for her, but then, it seemed to Danny, she was not happy no matter where she saw him.

(After some discussion, we've decided not to go into a detailed description of the Nurse or the way she treated Danny at this time. At the risk of taking sides, and aside from her Vet-like odor, I will say that, according to Danny, the Nurse's belly was hard to see over, and when he lay on the floor in front of her—"under her feet," she said, "every time she turned around"—he could not easily be seen. And I can certainly see how she must have felt uneasy as she moved about her job. Speaking of uncertainty and unexpectedness. E.T.)

As she clumped down the stairs, she was calling out: "All right, all right; I'm coming, I'm coming," and her voice had taken on the same high-pitched, frantic note that Danny's had. As she turned to him and commanded, "Quiet" in that same tone, a voice from outside the door pleaded: "Please, don't open the door now, lady, I beg you, please. I have the wheelchair here, and I need to slip it inside … but …Listen… Let's get hold of that dog first …?"

It was evident to Danny that the Nurse did not feel in control of the situation; she must have been debating whether to open the door or not—whether to open the door and have some unknown man torn to pieces before her very own, narrowly slit blue eyes—or to take hold of Danny's collar first, open the door, and then be torn apart on the other side along with some unknown man holding a wheelchair.

"I don't know what to do," she shrilled to whomever was within a hearing distance of eighty feet or so. "What should I do? I don't know what to do."

"You gotta hold onto that dog, lady. You gotta hold onto that dog's collar, like it was your kid's balloon. You hear me? Then, you open the door. That's all. You hold on and open the door. Let's get going; it's cold as hell out here."

(People are always saying things like "it's cold as hell" when most research indicates just the opposite of hell. E.T.)

"Well, I don't know. He could bite me. I don't know."

There was silence outside the door. Then, the voice said: "Try putting your right hand just lightly on his neck where the collar is." There was silence. "Can you do that?"

More silence, then: "Yes, I've done that."

"Okay, now listen carefully. You want to do this quickly, all at once. Listen first. You're gonna grab the collar, hold the collar, take your left hand and open the door wide open; hold the collar and stand back. Hold the collar and, then, close the door. You got that? Then, let it go."

There was silence.

"The collar."

There was silence.

"Lady?"

"All right."

She followed his directions exactly, especially for the first stage; she took the collar; she was nervous; she had no way of knowing Danny was only after the one outside. She opened the door a small crack; the man with the voice shoved the wheelchair inside fast, right under the Nurse, who sat down in it and let go of Danny's collar at the same time. But before Danny could get his balance or get around the chair, the man was back outside, and he closed the door.

In a short moment, a slip of paper could be seen sliding in under the door. As far as Danny was concerned, that slip of paper was just about as good, or bad, as the man himself would have been. The Nurse slumped down and out of the chair, onto her hands and knees; she held out a limp, unwilling hand to protest as she saw Danny approach the receipt.

"Lady?" Silence. "See that invoice under the door there? You just want to sign that paper of 'goods received' and slip it back under the door. Okay?"

Silence again.

"I can't do that." Her voice had lost its shrill quality and sounded as lost as a tennis ball in a brier hedge. "The paper is all wrinkled; it has holes in it, it's torn to pieces, it's wet, and I only have half of it."

There was yet another silence before the delivery man spoke. "I'm putting something in the mailbox. You can send it back later."

There were some sounds around the door; Danny growled under his breath. Then, there was silence again and quiet.

Danny wonders to this day how he sensed so much danger in that man and in the chair he brought to the house, but he did sense it. He knew, however, that he shouldn't have lost control as he did. In his life so far, losing control had never gained him the least advantage; in fact, it usually led to punishment—a nose whack or a confinement of some sort. His momentary lapse into wilderness behavior must have been caused by the presence of the Nurse or maybe the confusion in preparing for Christmas, disrupted schedules, strange events, and the like. And it did lead to confinement. When the Nurse, who was called Mrs Moolden, arrived in the morning to "help out," he, Danny Lunder, was shut in the den or in the upstairs workroom for hours at a time, seemingly forever.

(*At the last minute, Danny Lunder, proposed deleting this whole previous section because, he said, it had nothing to do with Jane and the letters, but when I was selected to edit the letters and provide a connective narrative between them, it was with the understanding that I would use my skill as I deemed necessary, and I believe this little scene at the arrival of the wheelchair reveals the tension in the household at the beginning of the following period of calamity; this event sets the tone for the next letter. E.T.*)

JANE LETTER #20

Dear Mahrowh,

I wrote in my last letter that Christmas seemed a time when all the peculiarities of life, the highs and lows, were condensed into a few days. But the last letter was mostly about the expected and unexpected *good* things that happened. There was the opposite too. The first thing I remember is that the Mistress took Maisie onto her lap while I was playing so wildly with the man on Open Boxes day. But that's really a small thing.

This is a large thing: Whenever she comes downstairs, the Mistress stays more and more in the wheeling chair I mentioned earlier, and when she is upstairs, she stays more and more in our bed. Something is wrong; she is different, and something is wrong.

Then, today in the afternoon, as the Mistress sat covered in the chair downstairs, for some reason Danny was let out of his confinement and the nurse was nowhere to be seen when the door bell rang. Danny began to bark as he does when other people come and ring the bell, and everyone says, "hush, Danny, shhh," and so on; then, the door opened and a number of extra people, all women, I think, came in and patted Danny until he quieted down, assured there was no immediate danger. As for me, just the sound of those clattering voices sent me to the foot of the stairs, where I paused and turned and heard and saw the Mistress say, "Oh, Jane, please stay a minute; it's all right. No one will hurt you, I promise."

And someone else I saw said, "I've hardly ever gotten even a glimpse of the new cat." Laugher and clattering continued, and I left—very quickly.

I went under the Mistress's bed. Maisie was on top.

Upstairs is lonely when everyone else is not there. I was reminded again of all that hiding and waiting I did alone outside. A little chill

143

ran down my back, just enough to lift a ridge of fur, and go on to expand my tail an inch or so.

In a while, Danny came looking for me; I could hear his nails clicking on the stairs before I could see him.

"They're not giving me any more cheese and crackers because of my weight," he said. "It's for my own good, but I wish it weren't." He gave me a lick and a nose nudge, which cheered me up a good bit. I ran about under the bed, from one side to the other; he tried to anticipate my moves; finally, he reached out and pushed my head down; I grabbed his paw, and we tussled around on the floor for a while.

It seemed like we were trying to recreate the excitement of what we did on Open Boxes day, but Maisie, who by now was draped over the edge of the bed, her two front paws hanging down to whack one of us now and then, said we could never hope to recapture the glories of the past. Still, we had almost as much fun because the dressing table chair turned on its side, and we used it to hide behind.

Later:

The house was back to its nighttime quiet state; the new people were gone, and we finally were served our supper. Danny ate almost none of his dry food. The man says that Danny behaved like a "true party hound," whatever that is, and Danny left to throw up behind the reading chair.

I do hope all these "holidays," as they call them, stop happening. And all these people, too many people, unknown to me, find other homes. Could I get used to having them here? My Dear Mah, not in all my nine lives.

So I wish for the same people and also the same quiet sleeping in a well-known place, for you and all cats,

Jane

JANE LETTER #21

Dear Mahrowh,

Oh, how my fears become reality! More and more people arrive each day now, a few at a time usually, but one night there were very many, and they stayed late. This happened about the same time that the man took off the remaining Christmas balls and then took the tree itself away, as Danny had said he would, and during this same time Danny would come in from his walks and shake water all over the kitchen and speak over and over of "how crisp and how invigorating" the air outside is. But inside, my fears increase. The Mistress is not in the kitchen at these times now, and the man has to wipe up the floor; he speaks often of having a "large back yard and a dog house," whatever that may be.

On this one particular night, the people, called "company" by the man, come late and stay even later; they sing songs like the Mistress does, but louder, and make many, many strange sounding shrill noises and pops. As I am crouching under the bed, my stomach rolls like a bubbling stew. Finally, Danny comes to check on me. He is as jolly as a wind-up Santa; the celebration downstairs excites him, especially when he describes bits of food, large and small, lying all over the floor, and I notice how he struggles to keep his tongue and drool in his mouth when he invites me to come down and try some. He says he has smelled most of these people before and they are definitely safe; they are even *good*, he says, like Masters; they offer him any food he wants and also rub his head. So then, before I know it, his head is pushing mine, encouraging me to move along downstairs with him. Well, his head moves too fast for me and he gets too close too soon, and, nervous as I am, without thinking, I reach out and clip his nose. I actually cause a little blood to seep out. Poor me. Poor Danny. He stops right there and blinks; he licks his nose. I give a little cry and put my paw out, this time with no claws on it; I touch his nose, I rub up to it. And then he licks mine as if to say, "It's all right, little friend. I'll give you comfort even if you don't accept it."

Dogs are like that, I think.

At last, everybody has left; they go out by the wheelchair door. The house is quiet again except for the low voices of the man and the Mistress in the kitchen. I come slowly downstairs and make my way to the kitchen. Danny lies asleep under the table; maybe, he has already eaten his nighttime snack. Maisie is nowhere in sight. I think I must be the only one still hungry. The Mistress sits, relaxed, in the wheelchair; the man hands her a bowl and a towel for drying; I run and jump on her lap into the bowl. She laughs. I feel damp.

"Jane's really a very clean cat," she says. "Cleaner than most dish towels, I bet."

"I'm not in the mood to fool around with cats, clean or not," the man says, and he takes the bowl away.

"Jane, you dear little thing." She rubs me all over. "How you seem to dislike so many people, I think, and so many seem to dislike you. There's no way to change that, I suppose, just as there's no way to change … many things."

"I don't dislike Jane," the man says. "I'm just tired." Then he kneels beside the Mistress with a wet rag in his hand, and he places his head on her arm, and she pets his hair over and over, along with mine.

He begins to shake, almost as I do when I purr, and the Mistress says, "It's all right, it's all right," something she says to each of us in times of fear.

I will go to sleep tonight with that thought.

Your "all right" right now kitten,

Jane

146

JANE LETTER #22

People and Nurses have not stopped coming yet; on the contrary, there seem to be more and more of them each day. At first, there was this one Nurse, this Mrs. Moolden, who came in the daylight. This is a person who, according to Danny, along with her pills, smells a lot like the vet. Well, that could be true for all I know. And then, if so, you'd have to say that everything here in this place smells like that place now.

Anyway, this Nurse spends most of the day bringing food and other things to the Mistress, and I spend most of the day hiding and waiting for her to go away—which she does every night, at first. At first, she would leave when the man came in, and I would play foot jump on the bed or string attack between the wheels of the chair. Sometimes, the Mistress would sing, "Oh, where, oh, where has my little cat gone" or other songs her Dad had taught her. Sometimes, she would press her thumb between the pads of my toes, and I would stretch way out, the length of my body, in pleasure.

Now, when the Nurse who calls herself Mrs. Moolden leaves, another one comes in; this one is called Gradilla. She smells the same. One night, I ran into the upstairs water room too fast. I leaped onto the sink hoping to catch a few drips from the man's toothbrush. "TaDa!" And then AAAhhhh! Gradilla screamed loud enough to send the water drops back up into the faucet.

The Mistress called from her room, "What's wrong?"

The man ran up the stairs: "What's the matter?"

Gradilla said, "Oh, my Lord, that cat! I think I'm going to faint."

"Please, don't do that," the man said. "Here…Let me get you a chair."

"I'm all right. Just get that cat out of here. I'll be fine."

But I couldn't be gotten out of anywhere because I was nowhere to be found for the rest of the night.

Danny loves his interaction with most of the new people; he interacts whenever he is let out of his confinement. Most people go "ouuy gooooy" over him and feed him samples of everything they eat, including something called "yogurt." But for us cats, the coming of the Nurses was the beginning of what we considered The Great Human Pollution. Now there's a man with the same pill odor who comes to move things like beds and chests around. And every day, we think it will get worse.

So, as I say, I am not handling the new people, the wheelchairs, or the strange smells well. Today, when I found Maisie sunning on the front window radiator cover, I asked her if she was made nervous by the people and the chair.

"My hair did get caught under the wheels … twice," she said, barely opening her eyes, "an occurrence I'd just as soon forget, if you know what I mean, dahling. As for the people, I'm completely happy without being cuddled and petted and fussed over anymore. If you really want to know the truth, I'd rather not have anyone pulling at my hair these days; I don't want to hear someone simpering away: 'Ooooh, look! Isn't she just marvelous; look how you can wrap that long, soft fur all around your fingers!' They call it fur, you know. You might think I'd be used to all that fuss, fuss, fussing, but I want to be alone now. Enough is enough, and I've had enough. All my young life I had it. You're welcome to all the touchy, feely you can find, my dear; as for me, a straightforward hair job, a brush with a gentle stroke once a week will do the trick." She sighed. "Must be getting old." She licked her shoulder twice. "Nothing is the same. The Mistress isn't the same."

"The same as what?" I asked.

"As she once was, for Lord's sake. As she used to be … as in the past."

Maisie thinks I don't understand her, and the truth is, I don't. She keeps repeating the same idea over and over, and that is not a clarification, is it?

"The same, you mean, in behavior, in how she treats you? That 'the same'?"

"Well, yes," says Maisie, "for one thing. And I don't like it."

"What does she do that's different?"

"Everything. Dahling, you must have noticed."

"Well I … I haven't been here … long." I knew at once I shouldn't have said that; it was not the best thing to say. "Murauwder."

"Exactly," said Maisie. She said that, and she licked the other shoulder once and then twice. She offered to compose a poem about it.

"About it now or before?" I asked.

Maisie explained that many poems involved both—that is, a recollection of something before the way it is now and then the way it is now. Poetry is not an easy subject.

"The way it was before and then now … would that be it?" I asked.

"My blue ribbons, dahling, what do you think? And it's not the same at all, is it?" She peered intently at her shoulder. "Hair is thinning. I think I'll just take a nap after all."

And I think, deep down, I didn't want to hear Maisie say that things weren't the same about her shoulder or the Mistress. I think deep down I knew she was right about both, then and now. Hadn't I sensed something was wrong? Is there more wrong than I know of? Is everyone and everything changing for some reason, and I don't know how or what it is? Dear Mahrowh, I will let you know as soon as I find out.

Until then, only knowing my love will stay the same,
Jane

BOOK I

Part Nine

In which Danny admits being so tied up with new company and treats that he overlooked serious evidence of household disruption and unrest:

Looking back, Danny can see that he missed some of the danger in the changes taking place with the Mistress. In fact, as Jane said, Danny loved having all the new people around, many of whom spoiled him, when he was let into their company, with extra treats—donuts and the like—and all of whom came in from the outside world wearing new scents, intriguing ones that he had never smelled before, and all of whom, with two exceptions, loved to fuss over him, rub his ears, and scratch his stomach. It was probably because he was so distracted that he missed many of the first signs of danger.

One exception to the good will accorded Danny glowered in the person of the Nurse who was called Mrs. Moolden, the one who did not appreciate Danny's efforts to protect the household, especially from delivery people. She kept herself very neat, very unwrinkled; there was always a lot of her neatly covered in white. She would tell you herself she didn't believe for a minute that a dog's mouth was cleaner than a human's, and since she was a Nurse, she gave as one of her guiding principles: cleanliness. Which goes equally along with the other principle, "godliness," whatever that is. And she didn't want a "filthy" dog around the "sick bed." In other words, as Jane wrote before, most of the time when either of the Nurses appeared, Danny suffered the indignity of being shut up in the workroom or the basement.

(Danny said earlier it was the den or the workroom, but when we conferred, he remembered that the upstairs workroom was called the den and that the other place was the basement. Be that as it may, I can see so often as I experience new lives and times how lucky we insects are not to be easily locked up, anywhere. E.T.)

Finally, it became clear, as Mrs. Moolden continued to go on and on about "medicine," that what Danny had suspected for some time was true: the Mistress was sick, and finally Danny knew he had to confer with Jane and Maisie.

"What is 'sick'?" Jane kept trying to understand many things at once.

"Well ..." Danny looked at Maisie for help.

"Dahling ...Haven't you ever been ill?"

"I don't know," said Jane. "I don't think so. Is it the same as sick."

"Exactly," said Maisie, and began to work on her tail.

"Well, I don't know if they are exactly the same," Danny began. "Let's see... It's when you don't want to eat and play. It's when you throw up but you haven't eaten any floor food, and you can't even eat boiled chicken afterwards, so you have to go to the vet. And your nose is dry."

"For both? For sick and ill?"

"Well, dogs overdo everything, don't they, little 'aren't-I-just-so-full-of-health-and-vigor' Janie? I know you've heard the expression, 'sick as a dog'." said Maisie, she, the crown of all queens. "Think masses of great, green drain pipe residue. I, on the other hand, can cough once or twice, throw up a neatly-packaged, rolled up hairball, walk away, and never look back, during or afterwards, fit as a fiddle, a new trip to the food bowl. Just like that."

"And I always eat and play," Jane added, "what's more, I've never been to the vet, so I guess that's to say I've never been sick or ill."

(Well, and, as a perceptive reader might conclude, the three of them never did clear up what, if anything, was being said; From what I can gather these conditions are bad or worse depending on the nature of the creature, but I, as a roach, am beginning to feel more and more like a stranger in a strange land, an outsider, an alien. In my family, again, though we die or are exterminated by the millions, it happens quickly, and we don't get sick or ill beforehand, at least not in a way from which we would ever be recovered by this Vet thing. E. T.)

JANE LETTER #23

Dear Mahrowh,

Who knows if you may have been wondering why I haven't written in so long, but our lives have been in turmoil here; the last few weeks have been fearful.

First of all, shortly after my last letter … (Well, it could have been as much as three weeks, cat time; I'm not sure … it seemed shortly after, but then, as more and more humans came in at every hour of the day and night, I lost all awareness of time. Day ran into night, and vice versa.) Well, the day I don't want to think of, well, it didn't seem fearful when it happened. It was just like another in the beginning, but then a few new people came and put the Mistress on an extra bed and took her out by the other door. And she hasn't come back yet. And that was some time longer ago than I can remember whether I consider it in human or cat hours. You might say the time "flew by," as the humans do, but that means fast moving, and I'd say just the opposite. I don't know. I don't know. And the only good thing I can say is that we have seen none of the nurses or other unusual people in the house for all these days either.

Since that particular day, Maisie has been more and more her nasty self than ever before. Wherever I go, she appears; she stares at me intensely; I wait to see how she'll move; I seldom rest. I know I am larger now, older and larger, so I don't always back away or hide; I just watch and worry. For that reason, we sometimes provoke ourselves into noisy scrambles at night. In the mornings, there are clumps of long Maisie hairs and shorter Jane hairs all over the rugs, and the rugs are scattered out of place. The man puts the rugs back without smiling.

Yesterday, somehow, a fight began in the daytime near my old love seat cave; it started just as the man prepared to eat the late meal.

He came running to us, waving his hands, a napkin in one, and calling out, "Oh, no! No, no, please! You two mustn't, please. Don't fight; don't bite each other. Please. STOP!" He waved the napkin near our heads.

We did stop. Water ran down his face; he spoke very softly: "My dear. Oh, my dear. You loved them. You loved them anyway."

Then, he was quiet. He put the napkin to his face. Then, he removed it and stood staring at the window as Maisie and I disappeared in our different directions.

Later:

Danny says maybe Maisie is lonely and sad, that even though she never did sleep by the Mistress's head as I did, she may miss some other warm part of her body. Danny says that he and I have each other but that Maisie has cut herself off from friendships and I should at least try to rub her cheek or lick her ear. I say *he* should do that if he'd like to. I say…Well, maybe we are all sad.

Meanwhile, daily events are ever more worrisome. The meal schedule is not the same as it was, and I know that for myself because I have been here long enough to know what happened before. Before, we had the canned food as a main meal and the dry for extra, as we needed it throughout the day. Now, for some time, since the Mistress left, the man has not put out our regular dry food ration. He has given us a morning dish, one half of an excellent, but small, can of chopped chicken, for example one day, grilled fish of some sort on another day, or liver pâté and so on, but then, afterward, even though I do a lot of leg rubbing, he continues to sit in his special, large reading chair most of the rest of the time; hours pass and he never puts out the two large dishes of kibbles we are supposed to have available during the daylight. Then, one evening, he doesn't even split another can of food for us at supper.

After two days of food deprivation, I tell you, Mah, I was hungry enough to approach the man as he sat in the reading chair. I rubbed against his legs and spoke most openly in desperation. With his eyes still on his book, he reached down, stroked my back, then gently pushed me away. I sat and stared. I had planned to get his attention.

I leapt into his lap. What was I thinking? I was not thinking. In a minute, I'll tell you what Danny had to say about my leaping, but for now, I can say that it did startle the man and caught his attention more than I intended. When his arms flew up in astonishment, his book slipped onto the floor along with me. Yes, I ended up back on the floor too, and, in fact, I'm not sure whether I came down of my own accord or along with the book or propelled by the man's hands.

He muttered something I wasn't intended to hear and picked up his book; he made his way to the stairs without looking back. It was bedtime anyway.

I know, I know. What a mess, and Danny saw it all.

"Look before you leap," he said.

"What about 'He who hesitates is lost'?" I said.

"Are you okay? Are you hurt?" He knocked my head askew with an affectionate ear lick.

"I have no broken bones," I said, "but I do still have an empty stomach, and I'm sick and ill of that. I'd almost rather have a broken bone." I paused. "I'm glad Maisie wasn't around."

"You should never jump into the Master's lap, Jane. I could have told you that."

"Too late, too late. I could have used the advice. But since you never got around to telling me in the first place, I did jump into his lap, as you saw, and a catastrophe has occurred, which, if I were hoping to blame on someone else, I could blame on you since you never did get around to telling me." I knew all along the truth. And I still picked a fight.

"Well, you've thrown yourself on lots of other parts of the Master with disastrous results; I thought you'd learned. Besides, you've never seen *me* jump into his lap; I thought you could figure it out yourself, put two and two together for yourself."

"Two and two add up to a lot more than four here, Danny. According to your records, you weigh 87 pounds. I weigh only … Well, I'm not sure of my exact weight, but it's a lot less than 87 pounds, isn't it? Maybe seven pounds?"

"That could be."

"So."

"So?"

"So, why would I think of my weight as being a problem in a place where you wouldn't put your weight? I mean, really, why wouldn't I put myself in a different place from where you do since I weigh a lot less than you do?"

Danny looked confused. "I'm not sure. I think you're reading too much poetry."

"Never mind. Anyway, it didn't work, did it?"

"Not as far as we can see yet."

"Yet?" There was a little pause here as I thought of what I couldn't see. And then the old sweetness in Danny's eyes softened me up to him as usual. "Well, it's not your job to be telling me everything I should know," I said. "But aren't you hungry? Don't you get urges of hunger all through the day?"

"You cats eat all the time, I know. We dogs usually only eat one main big meal a day. We control our appetites; we are healthy; we are reasonable; we eat what is served."

"Ha! And everything else you can find! You eat anything anytime anywhere in the house!"

Danny went on his way: "Then, we eat quickly and efficiently."

"You eat so fast the food flies in wet chunks all over the floor."

"Which we clean up."

"Leaving slippery, slimy spots. And when someone uses a paper towel to clean up those spots, you will eat that too, if you can get hold of it." Sweet eyes are often deceptive—or certainly not indicative of a mellow tongue. "Don't deny it. You'd really like to eat all the time too, wouldn't you, if you could, and if you could, you'd eat anything with an odor that you could swallow; you'd sniff out the rottenest, most putrid bodies and clothing anywhere in the world , wouldn't you?"

"Well getting rid of old stuff is helpful--"

"You have been seen eating the insides of shoes, not to mention the socks."

"Well --"

"Hair brushes ..."

"I can't help it if lots of things smell good to me. Besides, it's not all outside the range of normal food stuffs, Jane. You remember, just the other day, I found a carton of fresh eggs in the stereo cabinet, and I ate it."

"Carton and all, if I remember correctly."

"I found a half-eaten sausage in the laundry basket."

"From which you were very sick or ill."

"Yes."

I paused to reconsider, something one should do frequently in the midst of an argument. I licked in a space between my left front paw pads and did some biting there too. When I fell from the man's lap, some little irritant, some little piece of dirt or bit of rock must have lodged itself there. Also, this was the first time Danny and I had been irritated with each other.

I decided not to pursue this discussion further; I licked Danny's soft left ear, no softer than his right one of course...

But the situation here has put me in a mood of depression from which I am having trouble extricating myself and in which I haven't felt like "accomplishing" much of anything, even writing to you. But now I've done it, and I guess I feel a little better. Oh, Mah, where are you now?

Wish "food" for your hungry kitten,
Jane

(*This whole food discussion has left me with an uneasy feeling about cats, and a new feeling about dogs: it's a fact that dogs and we roaches are able and willing to eat a very large variety of non-traditional food stuffs in addition to the usual traditional selections, but I had never myself put two and two together to realize that we have that characteristic in common with each other more than most mammals and insects do. We seem both to stretch the term omnivorous in directions never even thought of, and maybe in significant ways, in ways unheard of or certainly unexplored in laboratories or academically. I'm not sure to what end research on the subject would lead, maybe knowledge for its own sake, but from what I read in the Times, we use grant money to study much more obvious subjects, like the project that showed how employees with windows in their offices did happier and more thorough work than those without. E.T.)*

BOOK I

Part Ten

In which Danny describes, from an objective viewpoint, the tension that arose between the household cats:

When he finished reading Letter #23, Danny felt even sadder about what sensitive parts of their lives he had overlooked when the upheavals began in that house, especially the stress at that time between Maisie and Jane. He regretted to think he might have calmed things down more, or even prevented some outbursts from ever happening at all.

(At this point, Danny gave me background information about Maisie and explained that he had originally been selected because he matched her in color, at least to some slight extent, but from what he says, that was the only similar thing about them. So much for having something superficial in common. As far as I can tell, the crux of the matter came down to one of everyday guilt: Danny thought he had let the humans down when, despite their same color, he could not become a friend to Maisie as had been intended. Now, at this time, considering you and I, Dear Reader, have never met Maisie in person, or, well, in cat, and she is not here to represent herself, we might wonder if discussion of this dilemma contributes to the story

161

importantly enough to keep or if much of this section should
be deleted as an unnecessary digression? Well, but how can we
know one way or another until we hear or read it? So, Dear
Reader, what else can we do, from my point of view at least,
but "wing it"? Please pardon the expression. ET.)

Anyway, from the time they first met, Danny had no doubt that Maisie would prefer to be the only animal for miles around, that he—and later, Jane, especially Jane—should be ignored, sent far away or something similar. Maisie would be ever so pleased to see herself exclusively displayed, draping her cream-and-chocolate-colored body parts over the edges of chairs and counters, shelves and tables, without a distraction in sight. And even though Danny lay pretty much quietly in the background by the time Jane arrived, Jane was a distraction; there's no doubt about that.

"But," Danny thought, "but what's life without a little agitation in it?" He might have said, if it didn't sound prejudiced and judgmental, that cats are more serious in the matter of disliking excitement than dogs are and that cats have more devious ways of punishing disturbers than dogs have. A dog will bark and jump around and let everyone in on the problem, but a cat will wait and wait and then send out a claw-filled paw just when everyone has forgotten about her. Yes, cats are good at vengeance. And waiting. But that does sound prejudiced and judgmental. Of course, cats don't seem to care at all what they are, he thinks, or what others think of them or that they might even have a fault to think about. You can say what you like about cats, he thinks, but they really operate on the notion that they are exactly what they should be and that the rest of us might as well spend our time, day after day, taking notes about how to make them happy. There's little introspection about it, just the knowledge that they deserve a peaceful, uninterrupted supremacy. And a good bit of their preferred kind of food.

But Jane was a kitten. And to Danny Lunder, she was a blessing, gladly allowed to be whatever she was. To eat whatever she liked. To sleep wherever she liked. And, he thought, with a wry grin, to disturb whomever she liked.

But now, to go on with the letters:

JANE LETTER #24

Dear Mah,

Since I last wrote you, situations here have only been getting worse. The man is just not …I was going to say "himself," but it occurred to me that I don't really know what he himself is. I do know he is not like the Mistress and that she has still never come back. I told Danny she must have gone to the vet, but he only cuffed. As for the man, left on his own, he sometimes feeds us and sometimes does not; sometimes, the food is fresh, and sometimes, it is not. As I think I said in my last letter, the first few days that he did not put out the daily ration of dry food, Maisie ssuffered hunger even more than I did, and as time went on, she grew ever more and more hostile.

Yesterday, or was it the day before? Well, recently she cornered me between the stove and the side of the refrigerator:

"So, look at tiny Jane; look at our sly little beggar of a housemate. I'd say she appears awfully well fed and healthy these days. How are you keeping your weight up, dahling, and aren't you even putting on a little bit extra if I'm seeing correctly? Does he give you special treats because he feels sorry for you, sorry for your appearance, so ugly and strange?" Her pupils became slits, and her ears tilted back. "I can understand his reaction, but I don't like it, do I?"

I stood my ground: "The humans do like my appearance; they say so; they say I have 'a certain clownish melancholy' about me and that I have many other expressions from different angles because of all my creamy blotches."

"Oh, 'creamy blotches,' is it? Now, doesn't that sound elegant."

"Well, maybe they've grown tired of the regularity of your perfect features, Maisie, after so many years."

"You little swish." Maisie took what can only be called a menacing step toward me. "How dare you make remarks about my features?"

"You may be old, but you certainly are never good-natured, never polite or kindhearted, are you?"

"So, it's not enough that you are eating large portions of food that should be mine by rights, but you go on to …You go on to disparage my whole … my whole … mind!

"I didn't mean to go that far, truly, but the part about eating food that should be yours doesn't make sense. What makes you think he would put out bigger portions of food for you if I weren't here?"

"It makes all the sense in the world to me, dahling. Think about it. He'd still have to open a whole can wouldn't he? And he wouldn't want to waste it, would he?"

"And are you telling me that before I came, you used to have a whole can all to yourself every day?"

"I am. I did. I'm almost positive I did. And I don't want to talk about it anymore. I feel faint." Still not taking her eyes from mine, she sat down.

I sat down too, still observing her. Finally, I spoke again.

"Danny says you might be lonely, and we might be better off if we worked up a friendly relationship and planned out a strategy."

"Danny. Well, of course Danny says that. He's a dog. What can I say? When he's lying down, he's licking something, but when he's moving around, he's panting with friendliness, throwing his tail back and forth, kissing up to everyone in sight. He's a relationship addict."

"So then, he knows what to do. Listen, I'm thinking of a plan." I began quickly to think it through. "Maybe one of us could be in the kitchen at all times, complaining and rubbing up against the cabinets, the chair and table legs, everything within reach, and the man's legs, too, whenever he comes nearby. We could take turns, have rotating shifts. We could create such sounds that the man would have to notice; he'd try anything to stop our noise and eventually, he would try food! He would remember and scoop out … the food."

Maisie looked at me; she and her tail grew still; her ears moved forward. "Dahling, I hate to admit it, but I can see us as a kitchen duo. I have an eclectic repertory of sounds. Yes! At this moment, I am creatively inspired! I will speak a poem, one that has been buzzing around in my head for several days now."

And here is what she said:

Bees

Success sometimes eludes us
When acting all alone.
To gain its great completion
Sometimes requires a drone.

We were quiet for a moment. Then, Maisie explained some important background information relating to the poem: "I admit that I've had little—perhaps no one on one—experience with bees, you understand. I am basing most of my observations on descriptions I've heard from Danny and on some delightful shows I've seen on the Nature Channel, but we poets know the truth instinctively and feel things intuitively, not just as they are, but as they should be."

"It sounds likely true to me, and not just for bees either," I said.

"Ah, yes, Little One. You are caught up in the concept of universality! Great art speaks to the masses, dahling, speaks to them all, yes, throughout history, no matter how humble their circumstances and so on; they will see the truth—bees or whatever."

"But if one hasn't seen a bee …?"

"That, dahling, is where the imagination comes in to play."

"Well, then, we need to begin; we need to play with our imaginations at once."

"Dahling, you must take the first round," Maisie said. "Since it was your idea, you must be experienced in it. I'll observe for a minute or two and then take my nap; that way, I'll be completely refreshed and ready to take my turn." Then, she turned away toward the main room. "Not bad, not bad," she said, speaking of the poem. "I will need to do some revisions and speak it again."

I said I would look forward to hearing it again. And she did repeat it later. She had revised only one line, fortunately. She went from "Requires a learned drone" to what you have above, very similar, which is why I am able to reproduce it here for you.

Meanwhile, I did take the first shift, from about 10 in the morning until 2 in the afternoon. When I went to remind Maisie it was her turn, I found her repeating her new poem over and over to herself, getting it ready for later.

> (*Danny tells me that Jane told him she was not sure which of Maisie's revisions had been the final one, the one included here. Anyway, as a sidelight, Jane told Danny that Maisie used poetic repetition to distract her thoughts from hunger pains . E.T.*)

Now, as I write this letter to you, dear Mah, I can hear Maisie in the kitchen doing her turn. She does make a lot of unusual sounds, but she is not nearly as loud as I am. I can hardly hear her in the hall. I imagine that show cats are not encouraged to develop their voices to any great extent. Sigh. So, for the present, I am not going to instruct her in methods of crying louder. I don't want to hurt her feelings or make her feel inadequate. I can mention the need for bigger sounds tomorrow, once she feels more comfortable with the task.

And so now, after all the ways we two have bothered each other, I'm so glad to see us working together at last. Danny was right. I feel hopeful about the future.

So, until the future, then, I remain your most imaginative, noisy and stormy gray kitten,
Jane

BOOK I

Closing

In which the narrator describes the dissolve of the only household he has known along with his own regression into a state of almost puppyhood:

The last letter helped Danny understand what might have happened to Jane. He says he can look back now and see also what might have happened to the Master. The noise and fighting between the cats had gotten worse; he knew that. What he didn't know or believe was how seriously the cats were being starved. Of course, Jane had told him she and Maisie were hungry, but as he recalled from days before, they were always on the edge of hunger, always traveling back into the kitchen, hopping up on their cabinet, nibbling off and on. He couldn't see what food was in the bowl. Maybe he should have realized the extent of the problem when Jane began to try pieces of his food at the evening meal. As he sat by the porch, letter on the ground, he struggled to shake off blaming himself for the past. "Do not cry over spilt milk," he thought; "lap it up quickly. Get your tongue cut." Well, enough of the past, the point is Danny could see how the Master got so bothered with and tired of the cat fighting that he was driven to a desperate measure: He put Jane outside.

His Master, to whom Danny was bound beyond a cat's understanding, must have thought Jane was the main cause of all the noise and fighting in the house because there hadn't been much noise or fighting before she arrived, and once he had read this last letter, Danny remembered also that Jane had been the one making the most noise during the kitchen negotiations. What he couldn't figure out was how, considering that Jane would not let anyone pick her up and had such a terror of certain crates, boxes, and carriers, was how the Master had ever gotten her to go outside any way. Danny had discussed with her these great container fears. Danny felt her trips to the vet would be 10 times worse than normal because of her heavy fear. But Jane had just said that she never intended to have to do anything whatever with the vet or whatever it was Danny was talking about. So.

But then, how did the Master manage to get her outside?

Food. It must have been her hunger. She was starving.

When he looked back, remembering this time, Danny saw that none of it was possible for him to understand: His Master had put Jane out on the porch in the cold without Danny... and without food?

It was during this period that he only got to see Jane outside during the times when he took his walks, and then, the Master would stomp his feet, shoo her away, pull on his gloves, and pull on the leash; it was cold, he said. Still, Danny and Jane tried to talk for short periods, going down the steps, walking a short way down the drive; she tried to follow him farther in his walk, and he tried to turn back and lick her dear little head.

He missed her so much.

Yes, this whole turn of events was hard for Danny to understand, and he spent long hours, especially when the Master was away, crying at the porch door. When the Master was in the kitchen, he thought Danny wanted to pee again.

"You just went out," he'd say or, "We just got back. You must be getting forgetful, old boy, like your old man." And he would laugh.

But the truth is he didn't laugh much these days, Danny noticed, and when he did, the sound came out as a harsh throaty gasp, almost as if he was making himself do it, out of habit. And the truth is also that few things were funny, and one of the things that wasn't was that the Master had become very forgetful, more forgetful than he realized, even as he joked about it, and that sometimes he took Danny out for the walks at unpredictable times, unusual time, too early or too late; Danny had no schedule he could depend on. In the end, before everything scattered, the Master often forgot altogether. Danny can hardly speak to tell of this period, of how he began to have "accidents" as the Mistress used to call them, in the house, the same as when he'd been a puppy.

(Because of the little Danny could or would say about this painful period, I have had to imagine some details to enliven the material in this next short section. But I can say myself I'm thankful we insects have such relatively uncomplicated toilet demands compared with those of the mammals I have known, especially the larger ones. E.T.)

The first time this sort of accident happened, it happened right in front of the back door. Danny had sat there waiting, crying. He'd scratched on the door, which by now had groves of scratches, like a roughly raked garden, almost his nail's length in depth. On this one fateful day, he began to feel too much pressure in his body to sit easily relaxed, compressed as he was into his haunches, so he stood up. At that point, of course, the pressure shifted and increased, became painful and then moved at once sharply down into his back left leg; he threw his weight to the right, and that was when it happened.

The Master hit him with a rolled up newspaper as he had at times in the past. Danny cried out, a single small, muted yelp; he backed away in confusion: humiliated and betrayed, yet wanting beyond all reason to do as expected by the one who mattered more to him than anything else. He simply stopped thinking.

(I have been thinking: the paper hit would have destroyed the whole of some of us, and I think it must have destroyed or damaged deeply some part of Danny Lunder. E.T.)

As the days passed, Danny began to urinate in all sorts of creative places, and it would have been funny if there hadn't been the humiliation and loss of trust. He tried to hide his other activity too, and he was fairly successful in these efforts. For one thing, Danny was strong. He found he could push large chairs away from the wall and insert himself behind them. Another favorite spot became the area at the far end of the pantry between, and then back behind, the clothes washer and dryer.

Danny will not describe these past days or speak of these embarrassments at present. Naturally, he became more and more ashamed.

Now, all this began happening at about the same time that Jane disappeared, the time that he didn't see her outside during his walks. But, as he told me, he also began developing a bad relationship with the whole concept of time altogether. *(These were not his exact words, but the general gist of them. E.T.)* And he became depressed. *(Again, my word, not Danny's. E.T.)*

It was also about the same time that a woman came and took Maisie away. Shortly after that, it was the time the boy began coming to take him, Danny, for walks. It was on one of these days that he found the little packet of Jane's letters, and he put them under the pad in his bed. Then, it became the time that one day, the boy came and took him to a different house.

The season had moved to days when the air takes on a breezy, youthful scent. It was one of those days when the door opened to a rough and confident rush of new wind, to a movement that stirred up the cold leaves and brought in scents of damp, heavy earth, yellow sprouts, and grubs—a day when a dog can smell all life in the making.

The boy came mid-afternoon and hooked on Danny's leash just as he'd been doing for some days or weeks now. But this day, the boy gathered up Danny's dishes and put them in his bed along with what remained of a large bag of food. Danny could smell the letters there under the bed pad along with the dry kibbles as he and the boy went out on the back porch as usual. The Master came out, too, and he gave Danny the long stroke down the back and said, "I'll miss you, Danny. You're a good boy."

Danny could not take seriously the latter comment. He knew he was not yet a good boy. Why do they always say that? And when will it happen?

He didn't know what "miss you" meant, but the Master stayed inside the house, and it wasn't until he and the boy rounded the porch corner and moved to a car in the driveway that he began to worry about something, not the vet, but... And he noticed a tremble in that back right leg as he paused beside the wheel. He'd smelled this car before from a distance and the woman who got out of it also before. She opened the car's back door, and Danny felt his uncertainty become fear, a kind of hot, liquid fear that spread wide across the top of his throat and extended with a quick, tight pull down along the back of his neck; he jerked away, claws gripping the sod, but the boy held him tight.

"Get in, Danny. Go on. It's okay. Don't worry. Granddad Jack will come to see you soon."

The first of many lies he would hear from this boy.

For a long time then, Danny lived apart from Jane, with his own troubles and in turmoil with himself.

BOOK TWO

BOOK II

Part One

*In which Danny introduces the reader to his new home and to
circumstances that led directly to a drastic move on his part:*

Danny quickly learned about the word "miss" and how it was
followed by someone or some thing that used to be nearby; he
learned that he missed Jane. And almost as much as Jane, he missed
the real Master and Mistress. He missed his house. The boy's house
was not like the Master's. There were no other animals. There were
only the boy and the woman. It was a big enough house, however,
and surrounded by a good-sized yard with a metal fence that stood
about twice as tall as Danny's back. And he did find the boy to be a
lively one and a good companion … most of the time and at first.

When they were in the yard, the boy liked to throw balls and run
around and stop and turn and then run after Danny. Sometimes, the
boy threw two or even three balls at once; Danny would run off in
all directions finally catching just one ball in his mouth; he would
turn then and approach the others, nudging with his nose, sniffing,
trying to figure out whether or not to drop the one he had and claim
another for his mouth. The boy would be laughing and sometimes,
while Danny was deciding, the boy would roll him on the ground
and grab his front legs and try to hold them in a way that had no

reason; it had no purpose as far as Danny could see, but he rolled around and over, too. He wasn't used to boys' play: he became a bit uneasy when he had no way to gage what response was appropriate in whichever game they played.

And sometimes, they played so long that Danny got tired. He wasn't used to lengthy periods of activity either. He lost weight, too. (He may have heard the Mistress saying that was a good thing really.) When he got tired, the boy would keep trying to play with him. He would smack Danny's face and nose from side to side and pull on his ears. That game was not at all in fun, and Danny wished it would stop. He'd growl because he wanted it to stop. Then, the boy would hit his head or whatever part was nearest and say, "No!" Danny would try to move away, try to hide, but the yard was almost empty. It had only a few of the boy's toys in it—a bicycle and a wagon, those kinds of things. There was no place to hide; he could only keep moving until the boy grew tired himself.

Danny was put out in the yard before and after school on weekdays, and usually, the boy remembered to put him out there at regular intervals on the weekends too. After a while or so, as he got used to the schedule, Danny carefully selected a place in the yard back along the garage side to use for his main eliminations, and he worked hard to quit having the accidents in the house. He did work hard at that; he knew the woman hated his "mistakes," as she called them. She had new carpet; he heard her say on the phone how it was just her luck that her father had "gotten bad" the very week after she'd laid in new carpet. She yelled "No" at Danny and shook his neck and made him smell his "problems." He tried devices like those he had used before at his home. But he'd grown so nervous that he made even more accidents. He'd feel an urge, and if he happened to think about the woman—or worse, if he got a whiff of her or a previous accident spot—he'd lose control. He continued his efforts to hide the problems, scratching up the carpets, trying to cover everything over, making space behind furniture. But after that, he had to try and avoid those places himself as well. The humans began to leave him outside for longer and longer periods; the woman went to work, and the boy came home from the school later now when he stayed to play baseball. Then, it turned out that the boy was too tired to play in the yard after the baseball. At first, when the boy brought the nightly meal of dry dog food pellets out, Danny would greet him with a ball for play; Danny would jump around; he'd reach out and pull on the boy's shoe, but as time went on and even though this was the same play as they had done before, the boy would shake him off and go back inside.

So, Danny was alone all day while they were away, and when they came back at nightfall, he was alone when they were both tired at night. Finally, there came a time when he was let in only for a few minutes, for a quick scratch on the head before they opened the door to put his food bowl out on the cement porch stoop. The woman said if he ate his supper out there, he would be safely out there to do his "business," as she called it, in the morning, and he'd not have to worry about making a "mistake."

"We don't want to take any chances, do we?" She placed a clean, folded towel, by the door outside for him to sleep on. Just until he learned to "control himself." She was always thinking ahead.

Some nights, Danny barked for company—until the woman blew a sharp whistle from the back door.

Soon, it became easier and easier for everyone if Danny took all his chances outside. They put his real bed and pad out on the porch. After a while Danny began to avoid the woman and the boy.

And after another while, Danny left the place.

It happened this way: One day in search of the spring sun, Danny left his bed on the porch at about the noon hour. He was carrying his packet of Jane's letters, as usual, ever so gently in his mouth. (He held them whenever he could, whenever he was alone; he loved to have them in his mouth, to feel and smell them.) He was moving haphazardly around the yard's enclosed boundary when he noticed that the boy had left the wagon, full of flat boards, next to the fence. The boards were supposed to be making part of a deck, whatever that is. The wagon was supposed to be stored beside the porch, but there everything was, resting right out in plain sight. Now, Danny is not a jumper or a climber by nature, but with the short lift he got from the wagon, and the other lift he got from the boards, he was able to half jump and half climb his way out of the yard, letters and all. He clung to spaces between the wires, reached the top, leapt, and fell to the ground on the other side; in a short moment, he stood, shook himself, and let out a squeak of a bark of delight between the letters. His belly was scraped in several places, but he hardly noticed at all.

At the time, he didn't stop to notice much at all. In those first free moments, he almost danced across the neighbor's yard, and then he took off in a gentle lope, traveling one way and another for several blocks. Finally, he came to a stop and lifted his nose.

(I, for one, do not know the complete powers of this particular dog's nose, so I am unable to give any details about what happened next. And all Danny knows is where, by way of his nose, he went. E.T.)

That first stop, that first designated street corner, brought scents to Danny's nose almost overwhelming in numbers and also in density and age; he received no doubt thousands of odors right there on that one corner; they were rolling into his nose, overlapping in repetitions and durations—some as old as years gone by, some as fresh as that very day. He stood with his head up and to the right, then front, then left. He lowered his head and released the letters, shook his entire body, and sat down. His collar was missing. How was that? And he shook again; his skin loosened and seemed to fall free, a whole inch or so released over his entire body, and he thought about the collar being a thing he didn't mind missing and then he thought how peculiar life can be. He shook his head to make sure it was clear, and swallowed freely. He collected the letters and set off in a trotting gait, more slowly now, to the left. He followed this route for an unknown time, nose up or down, one or the other, constantly checking high and low for new air movement and scents. In another while, he stopped and began to move to the right.

Using this method of progression, Danny came closer and closer to his old and original house, called home. And on the way, he encountered the usual kinds of distractions:

A car unexpectedly turning a sharp corner, fast.

A baby on a porch with a tempting cheese stick in its hand.

Probably 14 squirrels; various birds.

A crowd of laughing girls with ice cream cones.

Four dogs of neutral odors, on leashes.

A puppy wanting to play …

Those sorts of things.

At one point a woman approached him from behind and asked about the letters: "Hello there, you scruffy looking old puppy dog!"

He turned to look.

"Are you on your way … somewhere special? Home, for instance, or away from home, possibly? Come here. Come, come. I won't hurt you; maybe, I could help … no collar, I see. But could those papers you carry be of help to locate your family or friends …? Here … let me see … I have a little piece of … well, peppermint candy … in my purse and … maybe … Let me look… a packet of saltine crackers… You are bound to be hungry! But I'd say you don't want to eat a peppermint candy no matter how hungry you might be! Not peppermint. Let's see then … well, look at that … a fresh cracker! All right. Here's a bite! Nice cracker … Here you go; now, you just have to open that mouth and let me see the papers." Holding forth the cracker, she took two steps closer to Danny.

Maybe he was standing downwind of the cracker, or maybe he had gained a new wariness of people in general, but for whatever reason, Danny stepped back two steps and, turning, letters firmly in mouth, loped away at an easy pace, southward.

(*As we worked over this section, Danny apologized for forgetting so much about who or what he saw or where they were, or exactly how far he went during that afternoon, how many blocks or acres or miles he traveled. We've discussed how important details are to provide the reader with pictures of what happens. In this case, however, we have nothing more to offer, so I offer the thought that we'll likely come across a section where we'll find extra details later. E.T.*)

At some point shortly after encountering the woman, Danny caught a direct scent of his Master's house, and he slowed to a trot—at once, most confident of his direction.

He arrived at the front of the old house before nightfall. Every scent jumped up to catch his nose: from the sidewalk, from the grass and ivy along its edge, the birch tree, the Master's and Mistress's shoes ... He tore back and forth across the yard, down the driveway, to the back porch, soaking up the multitude of earth and animal scents he had been missing for so long, and minutes went by before he realized how much he missed them (There was that sad word again!) and then how old those so well-loved scents were now, those of the Humans and Jane especially, and he wanted so hard to believe they were just yesterday's.

New scents pretty much dominated the area, half covered the others. Between his lips and out past the letters, little questioning noises bubbled forth with every exhaling breath; he moved more frantically now, up and down the steps and around the porch railing. He moved quickly to the ground sides of the porch, back and forth, and suddenly there it was. He caught it. He caught a newer scent of Jane! He stopped. And knew it was hers. He slowed his movements, then, back and forth. She was under the porch! He heard a loud bark—his own bark. Letters all over the place. Never mind. Quite a few yelps. He began, yelping at each stroke forward, to half-dig, half-crawl his way through the bushes, to the side of the porch. He couldn't ... There were holes in the cross-cut strips of wooden barrier, but ... No. He couldn't push, or even dig, his way through to get underneath. Too big. He, that is. Despite all the exercise, the weight loss. "Cuff." A pause. Nothing. A deep breath. A sigh. With the intake of air he realized the truth, the missing truth, and he let the air out.

Jane was not alive under the porch. Nor dead under there. But... she... or something... of her...

Yes!

He should have been able to tell right away. He shook his head, admonishing himself.

Because, by then … his nose was telling him that something else… something like … Yes … just inside the latticework around the bottom of the porch, he touched several pieces of what appeared to be paper napkins and, then, something with the names and some scents of food all over it. He lay there, out of breath, smelling these things, until he began to pick at them and pull them out through the latticework. Papers. Jane's. So clear the scent. He laid them out next to each other in a row and took a long, deep collective sniff. After a while, he looked at them, each one … What he saw astonished him greatly since he usually learned much more from his nose than his eyes. What he saw was his name. This is what he saw: All the little sections of paper had his name at the top—his name, the name "Danny." They said, "Dear Danny," exactly as a letter would. They were letters. Letters to *him*. Letters from Jane to *him*!

(*The reader may feel that these last few mindless repetitions should have been edited out in a flash, but they weren't. E.T.*)

Danny could not take his eyes away from the letters . He nudged them all into a pile, and laid his muzzle on top; it was some unknown time later that he thought he would arrange them in two piles, those to Jane's mother and those to him. Of course.

Now Danny had not dealt with two kinds of written communication before, so he thought he would smell them over before going further. At this very house, when he had read Jane's first batch of letters, he'd never thought that some day she might write to him also or perhaps, as it seemed to be, exclusively.

As he sat by the empty porch, Danny sniffed the beloved papers in front of him until they were wet, so wet that even though he worked carefully to place each letter in its correct pile, some of the thin tissue-like paper stuck to his nose.

(*Fortunately, as I explained to him later, the writing was done with a ballpoint pen, and so most of the remaining words were legible, if not easily so. BUT after much discussion, we decided to duplicate the letters as much as possible in their original*

*condition so as to preserve the mood and tone of their authentic
time and place. (E.T.)*

When he finally sat back to read the letters, his tongue
automatically cleaned his nose of the wet tissue paper, much of
which ended up in his mouth.

*(Where he swallowed it. I've never been close to a dog before
this one, so I shouldn't generalize, but this dog eats a larger
assortment of materials, other than dog food, than any other
mammal I have EVER known. And I thought we* Blatta
orientalis *were multi-omnivorous! Again I marvel at what we
have in common. E.T.)*

He selected the top letter and waved it a bit to dry. On the one
hand, when he began to read, he saw it was still not easy to make out
the exact meanings. On the other hand, he thought, well, anyway,
it's the gist of the matter that's important in the long run.

JANE LETTER # 25

("In the long run" this or that "hand" can wipe out all the matter when the terrain is rough. Unlike some earlier letters, which could have offered more detail than necessary, here, in some of these later letters, the material provides less information in a more difficult format than you, Dear Reader, might prefer. Still, I hope you will persevere despite the difficulties. E.T.)

Dear Danny,
      Oh, how I miss your warm yellow presence and
How I fear of never
again.   I went back to   you weren't
there.

Yet when   and the sky is   blue and
warm,
I am   and sure   good nose   find
this letter. I

regret how much in life one cannot   but then I think
if we did know
ahead
we might despair   By the time you do read
I

will most
not be   in   this disappointing   where I
have
waited and waited and
for   a word of friendship

You know how I cannot   be picked up or also
a   box
So   In the end,
food was   and   lured me outside again.

*(Danny says he does know and remember all of this, and when he read
it, he put his nose between his paws and closed his eyes. I don't know
why. E. T.)*

the best canned food. Tuna and shrimp pate I
think   My nemesis   before   don't want to deal with

go wherever it is   out on the porch   door shut
hiding
cold   you gone   no   or walks.
Oh

          to take back some actions from the past
good as
see ahead   in the first place?

              under it again   wondering at strange
        sounds   and   much of the
        day.
man did put   food   filled to the top   off
and
                      for a while

couldn't eat it all, but someone did,   the raccoon

                    Double00 maybe   last
              days
then   forgot   now

my   hum   mans   now   gone   too

182

But, dear Danny, and I know you will not f or get no matter where you are.

(Dear Reader, you will be happy to see some undamaged stationary in this next section of the letter. E.T.)

And speaking of animals who eat cat food, I talked to that big old yellow guy the other day. He told me his story, and although it too involves making a decision without knowledge of its outcome, a decision one might come to regret in some ways, at least in some of its ramifications, I think he would not change his decision; I think he would do the same thing again.

When I saw him, he was shut into the porch next door. This place was surrounded by a strange sort of material that I could see through, smell through, and hear through, but when I tried to jump through, I was snapped back short and popped in the nose. I reached out to grab on and my claws caught into some little holes there. Yes. That was a surprise. Then, the rather hefty feline who was lying on the table turned to look at me and flopped his tail a few beats.

"Yep, is that you?" I asked, holding on, looking at his spot of sun on the table and the bowl of food by the door.

"Well, hey there, little sweetie! Lookie here, do I know you!? Listen up. Yep, let me tell ya: ya gotta lay off yer hold onto that screen mesh there wit yer claws. Let that stuff go right pronto now, Lady. Hanging onto that stuff can get you into big trouble around here. I am not kidding you, kid." He rose up in bulk and sort of slung his way over to the edge of the table.

"I'm stuck it looks like."

"You come unstuck mighty fast enough when they hit ya with the water bottle spray."

"Water spray!" I was trying hard to release my front claws, but one of them was being pulled so hard down by the force of gravity, as they say, that I couldn't disengage it.

"Hold on," he said; he stopped and gave me a straight-on stare. "Lookit you here! Haven't I seen you somewhere before?"

"Well, of course you have, Yep! I mean, Tom... I'm the one you met-"

"Are you the dainty little thing used to live under the porch next door? Ate the food out there on my porch, too?"

"Well, once in a while I did eat-"

"I hardly recognized your form! Don't you look plump and shiny ... very nice, very healthy."

Meanwhile, my plump and shiny body was dangling in the air, hanging from a single claw, now tearing away at the hole it was caught up in. Finally, I was able to grip with the back claws enough to contract the front one and drop free down to the ledge around the porch. I checked my claws for damage, then looked back to the table where Tom was stretching out his back.

"You're looking ... healthy too," I remarked. When he jumped down from the table, I could see fat pouches lobbing back and forth under his belly. In truth, I think he'd grown a little too far beyond the healthy side, but I don't think one should begin a conversation with someone she hasn't seen in a long time by making that kind of honest remark.

"So, somebody liked those fluffy cream splotches all over your body and took you in for good." He sat nearby and checked out his own foot pads too, almost in sympathy for me. "Gave you a home of your own."

"I had thought so," I said and tried to stretch out then, along the narrow ledge; I managed to sit down before I fell off. "Now, I find I was mistaken about that."

"How do ya figure?"

"I don't know exactly," I replied; "I lived with them some months or so... Well, it's probably a long story." I gave a soft muurr. "But I see you have gotten your own place now, your own home. I hope you can be sure."

"Little gal, you better believe it."

"That's good."

"Not without a compromise here and there, some sacrifices along the way, if you get my meaning."

"Oh. I guess we all have those."

"Listen, little gal, you may remember that, in my youth, I had a humongous set of-"

(I assure the reader that, again, pieces of the letter were missing here much as they were on the first page although Danny Lunder thinks I have deliberately cut them out. E.T.)

"... so, as I say, I must be missing some of my body parts. I don't feel my special bounce back there anymore. Course, everything could just be shrinking up with age, I guess. Say, Little Cutie, I wonder if you'd mind taking a look for me, tell me what you see ..."

With that, of all things, he turned around and showed me his rear end. Well, I didn't have much in my experience to compare it with without being indiscrete.

"To be truthful," I said, "other than my litter mates and mother, the only cat I've seen intimately is Maisie, and she's... Well, you know."

"Never mind," said Tom. "I have a feeling about the latest trip we took to the vet. I have a feeling that I may have had my last contact with my intact tomhood. I have a feeling I may be Tom now in name only."

"Maisie says, 'What's in a name?' She's a poet."

"I didn't know that."

"Yes, she is."

"And what is a 'poet' if I may ask? Does she like it?"

"Let's see ... it's, um ..." I hesitated because I wanted to be careful to explain fully, not to discredit Maisie. "It's one who thinks up the words that will tell you exactly what you know... better... so you can hear the things that you've, um, the things that you've actually known, better."

"Yeah? Well, good luck to her is my comment."

We sat and looked out for a few moments.

"You look happy and … rested anyway." I didn't want to appear intrusive.

"It's not so bad when you take it all in all. Quiet. A peaceful, predictable life. Not many challenges. A little standoff about the amount of canned food provided. That kind of thing. Not like the old days when everything was up in the air."

"I know."

"They feel sorry for me, you might say. With my many life scuffles. Lookit this." He inclined his head to show me his chipped up ears, turned around to present his crooked tail, then sat down again. "They make me take it easy. Hey, I learned how to purr again. You know? After all these years."

"Oh."

"Maybe in times past, I'd of called a life like this boring, but I'm ready for it now. Nobody's getting any younger, you know what I mean? I mean, we gotta think of the future, find a place to live out the aging days."

The turn of this conversation made me so sad that I could only look away.

"I mean, when you're young, you can go for more than you've already got, but us old guys need to hold on to just about whatever we end up getting. Came to the point in those stormy days last fall, in those days when the cat-pellets that the humans put out in their plastic dishes bloated up like soaked croutons, when you couldn't swallow any more of the slimy blobs, when you couldn't get your soggy cat body dry after it made its nightly rounds… Well, I came to the point of being fed up or … more likely, of not being fed up … Got it!? Maropah! Do you call that poetical? Well, anyway, on top of all that, this steakhouse I frequented on weekends just up and crashed without a warning. Yep. Closed right down. Went to empty. First they had this big blast around about Turkey time. Liver and gizzards coming out the door by the platters full, I can tell you; then, by Sunday night, empty as a Cicada shell in August: windows closed, not a sole in sight, no lights, no cars, and not even a garbage can with last minute throwaways. And there was December looming up ahead, the rear end of half eaten rat.

"One day soon after, it was raining as usual; I was sitting like a used-up floor mop under those bushes right there, right below where you are now, and the humans were out here on this very porch, this very dry porch, she with a bowl of food in her hand, he holding the door open. Well, the time seemed planned; it just seemed I had been chosen, so I went on in."

"And you've been here ever since?"

"Oh, I might go out, I reckon, but you know, all in all, it in't hardly worth the effort. Down the steps and up again, all that. I get the sun right here. Yep."

"And food too, as you say."

Tom gave me a sideways look. "I bet you never did eat grub of the street, never did take my advice, did ya? You know, a cricket spews bigtime protein."

"Well, you see, I went inside too, pretty much the same way you did," I said, thinking about what is now gone.

"Well, I'm glad you did! And look at the little lady, in fine fiddle and with a new home to boot. Yep."

"It's true. I did have a ..." I just couldn't say the word, and I looked away. I was too upset even to lick my shoulder.

"Seems like you're losing a lot of homes and not being able to speak of the sorrow connected with the homeless. Why, I remember when I met ya back then before, you were in sadness about another lost home."

"I can't believe you would remember that!" I was again amazed at such a revelation.

"Listen, honey babe, in those days I remembered just about everything there is to remember about a sweet looking little beauty like yourself."

"I don't seem to be having much luck with homes. I've lost two so far, and I don't think I'm even a year old. You don't suppose the humans here, the ones where you are here, would feel sorry for another, but smaller, cat, do you?

"Well, now, ya know, I don't think they really-"

And just at that moment, as in so many of life's stories, the woman Tom had mentioned earlier appeared at the door and then came onto the porch as if to be prepared to answer the question herself.

"Should I meow and do rubbings against the screen?" I asked.

"Not for now," Tom replied. "I'd hold off on your approaches for now... See how the fur lies ..."

"Jason!" The woman spoke to Yep, that is, Tom, as if his name were Jason. "What in the world have you got going on out here? I thought we'd taken care of this problem at the vets..." Then, she turned to me and flung her arms and hands wide about like a confused pigeon. "Shoo! Shoo!"

I tried to make myself look forlorn, pathetic, hungry, and yet attractive, playful and friendly at the same time.

"Go! Go away, you strange-looking little cat! Move. Move on. Shoo!"

I tried a soft meow.

"Get! Get away!" shouted this woman, and the next thing I knew I was hit in the eyes by the very squirts of water Tom had spoken of. And I saw Tom himself, well out of the way, shrinking behind the rubber tree plant.

Well, I did "get away" from that porch and that human and in a jiffy, too. Fear and humiliation can bring about quick changes in one's agenda and, depending on circumstances, cause new, unexpected behaviors in carrying it out. I tripped and fell on my chin as I left the porch ledge.

But I was ready to be anywhere else but there.

As I left, I looked back at our old house. Where are you, Danny? Could you be lost now, too? Where is the man you walk with? Tell me where I should go!

I will continue to write you, if possible. I can only say how I do miss your big cold nose and humiliating tongue. Your soft ear.

Jane

P.S. After this last conversation with Tom, I did keep my eyes out for crickets and other moving insects. My conclusion is that, protein or none, they're hardly worth suffering through the scratches left on the inside of one's mouth and the stomach pains caused by their indigestible skins. If one ate enough of them to survive, if one could find and catch enough of them to eat enough of them to survive, one wouldn't want to survive, not with the pain, not with the damage done to the internal organs.

(Speaking of suffering, we Blatteria *have suffered complaints about our exoskeletons too: Our household enemies dislike the sound of them crunching under their shoes. I say, "Viva la crisp shell!" For me, the grass is not always greener on the other side of something or more exactly, on the inside of it out; I could not survive the outer covering of squishy, thin unprotective softness that so many helpless creatures endure, and if these others could only walk a mile in my feet, they would understand why.*

But to resume: We see that the next letter to Danny comes again on some unconventional stationary. The front of it is written on what appears to be a menu from an eating establishment where Jane had taken up residence.

I do encourage you, Dear Reader, to persevere, to endure the constant interruptions and not to skip this page. The touching sentiments at the conclusion will be even more so after you have endured the torturous confusion building up to them. E.T.)

JANE LETTER #26

Dear Danny,

Do you remember I told you about the night I watched old Double00 use a coat hanger to raid a **Roasted Portobello** garbage can behind Kelly's restaurant? He wedged one of the triangular ends up under the lid and pushed the whole **brown buttered** top off. Well, after a while, after sitting around a while, I realized that hanging out under, or on, somebody else's **smoked** back porch, no matter how familiar, wasn't leading to a life of any meaningful **cooked to order** sort, and I began to follow the food routes Jake and I had used in the old **pickled** days. I was managing to get by with a mouthful of hamburger **in a creamy dill sauce** here and various bits of **deluxe California style** chicken there when I began to notice old Double00 again.

So, by the next week, I was **in a red wine sauce** watching and following Double00 everywhere, although I missed my friend Jake all along; I was eating what was left **on the half shell** around the different garbage cans that Double00 frequented and thinking I'd be able to gain more **hot and flaky** information about additional locations of **authentic Italian** food and, perhaps **for an extra $1:00** shelter too. You see, when I went back to find my old **blackened grilled** place to sleep, that box in the shed where I'd spent those first few **piquant** weeks with Jake underneath, was gone; in fact, the whole shed **baked or sautéed** was gone, not a trace left, the ground all smoothed across and covered with what probably were grass seeds and weed killer **au gratin**.

Meanwhile, I discovered that Double00 had an uncanny awareness of what was safe and what was not as far as humans were concerned, and he played games with everyone. He knew which people overfilled their cans and which put leftovers out in bags beside the cans, which were too lazy to open the lid but did lay the bags on top, and which left the lids half on. And although, as I said before, I have seen him open a can on which the lid had been fully, tightly lowered, such a process took up precious time, and I kept thinking it might be all for nothing ... unless he had a terrifically discriminating sense of smell. Well, he did. And the times he opened such a can, the rewards were great—fish or seafood of some sort usually.

You may not know this, Danny, but these were the days when garbage cans stood about two dogs tall, were very climbable, and had lift-off tops. I often worry that humans will figure out how to improve upon these cans in some way, make them larger, perhaps, and with lockable tops so that Double00 and I and our kind, lost or left or born in the wrong places as far as humans are concerned, will not be able to use our wits and survive. I shiver to think that the future of everything lies in the hands of these creatures who have both the capacity and the audacity to improve anything the way they like.

And they're so unpredictable in what they like.

Anyway, it would seem a shame to lose such a spirited animal as Double00, one with a true devil-may-care attitude toward adventure and fun, just to secure more garbage. At any rate, we had some narrow escapes; you can imagine.

One such incident occurred just at dusk on the first night I went out with him: We made our approach around behind an old brick house with a porch in the back, and before I take cover I see a large human male pushing himself back and forth in a sort of swing-like thing and looking all around the yard as he does so. It seems as if he catches sight of Double00; he rises up in bulk, pulls open the house door, lets it bang shut, and shortly comes out with a plate of freshly cooked chicken parts which I could smell from my position by the garage corner. As I watch, the man makes his heavy way down the steps, pauses, then places the plate on the walkway to the garage and lugs himself back up onto the porch. Well, you can imagine my delight as I eye this openly unattended plate of pure, recently grilled chicken. And you can imagine my confusion as I watch Double00 scout along the edge of the yard in his usual jaunty style, then stop at the sight of the food, then sit down in the shrubs, then continue to sit and sit and sit and never move to the food. I sit down too, right by the corner of the garage; I sit down, but I just can't wait very well. I smell the chicken, warm and greasy. Before I really think ahead, I'm creeping out from beside the garage, around the garbage can, and up to the plate. It is fresh chicken all right, thick on the bone, large juicy hunks, and I select a leg, maneuvering to get a grip strong enough that I can hold it and retreat to eat behind the can.

The sound is a pop, like the sound of a wine cork being removed, and the feeling is a sting on my left ear. The laughter is a sharp crack and a cackle, something like the crowing of a rooster past his prime; it fades away to silence almost at once. And I leave at once, too, empty jawed.

Why Double00 kept coming to this yard, I couldn't see, until one night a couple of weeks later. We were all sitting there: I well out of sight by the garage, impatiently waiting to move on, Double00 in the shrubs, as was his way, and the man on the porch, as indicated by the creaking sound, was lopping back and forth in the swing thing. I heard a ring from inside the house. It took me only a second to remember the sound of a telephone. From what I've seen, most humans can't resist the ring of a telephone, so I was not surprised to hear the door slam and the swing jerking to a slow stop. And then, pretty soon I hear a voice getting louder inside and a strange clicking sound as the door opens again. I look around the corner to see Double00's tail sliding into the bushes, the meat plate empty behind him. Five or six popping sounds cut the night, pause, hang in the air and drop. But I don't feel any sting this time.

(Danny tells me that Jane told him that sometimes the chicken man only pretended to go in and answer the telephone and that in order to grab the chicken, Double00 had figured that he had to first, hear the door slam, then hear the voice of the man speak inside and then hear the silence as the voice inside the phone spoke and then hear the chicken man speak again in reply, and pause again, and so on. That raccoon knew more tricks than

192

anyone could stash up a sleeve. Danny also tells me that Jane would never have spoken with, much less developed a friendship with, this raccoon because her opossum friend Jake had severely warned her against raccoons. Why, I don't know. What is it about mammals that makes them always turning against this one for that or that one for this, this, that, and the other and always trying to figure out who it was said or did what to whom or why or why not. What I do know, because of what comes about later, is that Danny was right: Jane and the raccoon never did engage in a "bonding moment" if I understand that current relationship terminology correctly. E.T.)

So, over the days, while I traveled a good 15 dog lengths behind him, this raccoon led me to various satisfactory food sources, and the best of them, for me, turned out to be the back of the restaurant upon whose menu and napkins I now write. I think it's a fancy place, judging from the dishes listed on the menu; these are foods no simple alley cat is used to tasting, but the people who bring them out hardly ever latch the garbage cans. I've decided to take up residence here, while being careful to keep hidden at all times.

There's a plank loose on the side of the wooden garbage platform; if I push it with my head or paw, I can slide it up and over far enough to crawl underneath. Come and find me here whenever you get this letter. You have to go across the big street, the one I think of as Dead Street, so turn right just past Kelly's and cross the side street first. Stop at the restaurant with the awnings, go behind it, and give a bark. I'll be waiting and listening.

The weather has been milder these days, so the need for warmth is not as desperate as when I was first closed out. Sometimes, though, the wind grows anxious in the night and the little loose plank shudders and sighs beside me like a door that would like to open. Sometimes, I shudder and sigh too, even if the wind does not touch me.

> But always I wait for you to come here, and I remain your own special cat,
> Jane

BOOK II

Part Two

Dear Reader, the next section of narrative contains some material that might be considered offensive by those who are easily offended by the truth, but anyone else should find it unusually educational. E.T.

As Danny reads his letters, he completely looses control of his tail (which goes on to sweep out a good-sized isosceles triangle in the dirt beside the porch) and his voice (which goes about making rapid sounds of anticipation but in tones of uncertainty). That's what can happen with the promise of great happiness, he thinks, as he struggles to slow everything down: It is just a promise, a daunting possibility that could or could not occur soon or much later, or, perhaps, not at all. Danny sighs. He shifts on his haunches, settling into his hips, then extends his forelegs and slowly lowers both shoulders to the ground.

Jane could be close by.

There is a pause; then, his nose finds the two stacks of papers again as if they were knapsacks of newly shot pheasants and there was no hunter in charge. He comes to within an inch of the letters; he twitches; his whole body responds in wild excitement and before he knows it he is chasing himself all around the porch, then up the steps and down, barking without shame. When he finally stops, his energy is spent. And there are specks of blood everywhere; his tail had hit the railing with excited force wherever he'd been.

"I'm just never calm when something unbelievably wonderful may be about to happen," he thinks. "And now look what I've done."

> (*At this time Danny wanted to discuss his tail, which discussion I felt would be either irrelevant or in poor taste, probably both, and certainly destined to retard the forward movement of the plot. I did agree to inform the reader, however, that this sort of bloody tail injury is not unusual for Danny or for other enthusiastic long-tailed dogs; it is not a thing to be worried about, as a rule, although there are certain cases in which death could result. E.T.*)

To help gain self-control and to extend the time needed just to consider the, or a, possibility of such an unexpected great happiness, Danny decides to clean up his tail, a decision that leads to some extra work on the other parts of that same region and a kind of slowdown, a kind of tension release. But sooner or later, he knows he has to deal with the letters, first to read them again, especially the directions to Jane's restaurant. "But there is your nose," he thinks to himself as he licks away; "forget the so-called directions." "No, no," his other self says back"; the directions will be more exact, maybe even quicker, and besides if Jane went to all the trouble to write them out, the least you can do is to use what she's written."

So, the time sped by as he reread the letters, and then soon, there was no time left except to make some decisions. Should he hide one pile or both or carry with him one or both? He lowered his nose, whimpering. He raised his head, and he stood up; he stood fast and firm, and with all his strength he resisted the temptation to push everything out wide over the ground, helter-skelter, then dig it under, or maybe scratch and snort it all up into a pile, then lie down on top and roll back and forth, to maneuver so that every scent covered every inch of him, so that every scent became a part of him.

(*Danny has explained to me how the hunting dog is trained and worked. I remember the explanation well; late one night, when we had both eaten, Danny grew busy washing down his meal with a few laps of water ... Well, no, that sounds too refined; actually, he was sloshing and slurping down as much water as remained in the bowl, and when he looked up and began to speak, water, along with heavier threads of drool, began refilling the empty bowl. I was balancing five legged on the rim of the food bowl in a frustrating effort to wash and wipe my sixth leg. I know most humans have no idea how carefully the average roach maintains him or herself, but take my word, it isn't easy. Well. So, I'm not sure what brought the subject up, but suddenly Danny shook his head, and, Dear Reader, you would rather not know where all the cascading waterdrool landed, elsewise, you would be unable to eat in a kitchen where a dog has been living, but he shook his head and said that hunting dogs prefer to eat their meals from dishes; he said that hunting dogs are not comfortable eating directly from the floor or ground because that would be where the "prey" would normally lie; he said such eating conditions would be disruptive to the training. I felt some discomfort here myself, and then he went on to say how the retriever type of hunting dog, such as, he reminded me, he is, has an unusually gentle way with his mouth; he can carry around even the most delicate prey without killing it should it be unfortunate enough still to be alive, without even crushing or wrinkling it. During training, he told me, some dogs are required to carry around an uncooked egg, in its shell, in their mouths for longer and longer minutes of time so as to teach their mouths the exact touch they will need not to crush the prey.*

"And also not to eat the egg," I said.

Danny cocked his head at me as if to say "that should be obvious," and then he continued: "The setters and the pointers, all they have to do is to show where the prey is; they don't need to worry about crushing or eating it." He changed the subject.*

"Of course, they want to eat it. Everybody wants to… eat it. So, there's another whole side of the process that has to do with training the nose and teeth."

"How do they train the nose, then," I was interested. I have an excellent nose, all untrained though it is.

"I don't want to talk about that," he replied. "Maybe I don't really know; let's just say I don't really know, but we could just say it can get pretty violent, pretty unhappy."

We both sat still for a while, thinking of all the violent unhappiness creatures suffer.

Then, Danny said, "They probably smack the nose."

"Smack" is a good word and I thought that too; I thought they probably do. That would be the quickest way.

"To keep it from wanting to eat the prey," he explained.

"Well. But I hate to think that the purpose of all the training then, all this delicate and violent instruction, is to keep the nose and mouth of the dog from wanting to eat what the nose and mouth of the hunters want to eat."

"That's got to be the idea, you know, unless they just want to do it for fun."

"Well," I said, "we all like fun."

Danny soon regained some of his usual perky style and put away the thoughts of being hit on the nose. "Retrieving," he told me, "has to do with charging around into the bushes or grasses and finding the right body and bringing it back. Sometimes, the body has landed in water. That's the most fun of all, water. I can go in and out of water for hours. You'd have to put a leash on me to make me stop. I bet."

"You don't say," I said.

"Don't you believe me?" he asked.

"Of course, I want to believe you," I said. And I asked him what sorts of bodies there'd be out there in the water to keep the average retriever wanting to carry them around for hours.

"Retrieving," he says, "not carrying. Retrieving is the word and it would mean bringing back the different items shot down by the man with the gun. *Different bodies of interest. Usually, a bird of some sort, I believe; maybe a duck. Different things"*

Then, Danny was quiet, and next, he lay down and placed his head on his front paws, and he said he had never retrieved a real bird.

"I've never been a retriever at all," he said.

I thought to myself: not to have ever been a retriever ... It must be a very disappointing thing for Danny to think of, might even seem like a failure as he thought of it, but I had to say to him, as my own honest thought, what I said: "My friend, I have never met a bird myself, have only read about them and seen the pictures; I've seen how they fly, so far up in the air, with their wings out wide, with nothing holding onto them, nothing even close by. I'd hate to think of one of them falling down here, to be carried around in the mouth of a large dog, even a gentle one like you Danny. So, I would say that you are better off not being a retriever."

"Not being what I am?"

"As Jane said once, think of Maisie. What's in a name? Turn it inside out or learn to retrieve something else, maybe a ... a newspaper ... or ... a-

"Tennis ball," he said, somewhat resignedly.

"Why not!" Even as I said it, I knew I didn't understand his existential angst, the depth of his longing, and I had to acknowledge the limitations of my life experience as a roach, more reading than doing.

I decided to encourage Danny, to tell him how well he had learned to use his mouth for the good things he did, things besides retrieving, how good it was for him to use it as he always had, for cleaning and comforting himself and others, for carrying letters . What are our real choices, after all? What else could I do? E.T.)

After licking a drop or two of new blood from his tail, especially the tip, Danny took one last look at the directions to the restaurant.

Then, he gathered all the letters and all the pieces of letters, both old and new, into his careful mouth and set out on what he hoped would be his last lonely journey.

It was not to be so.

As he turned to cross the street where the humans were sitting behind a little black fence and moved over toward the awning restaurant, he knew something was not right. Something was surely wrong. For one thing, when he passed across the street, he caught no new food scents such as should have been leaving the awning restaurant ahead and mixing with those that had been surrounding the fence restaurant behind; from another standpoint, he simultaneously noticed the lack of sound in front of him. By this time, in early evening, both places should have been roaring with sounds, not only of human voices, but of plates and other things like that and music. There were no sounds or scents in front of him. No one sat at a table under the awning. And then, he noticed that the awning was torn.

He held back a number of barks until he'd made his way around to the back and seen the empty place—all quiet, unused, with some stale French fry grease spilled on the cement under the garbage platform and just above that, a little loose wooden plank swayed forlornly in the dusk.

But Jane had been there. He knew that, of course, and not so long ago either. He was not always clear on the timing of scents that were, say, over a few weeks old but under six months. Well, the time had never seemed as important as the identification. But maybe it was important, he thought, in a way he hadn't realized before. Then, he thought, "Oh, well, never mind. No use to cry over spilt milk, as the Mistress used to say." But then, he'd never done that. He'd drunk it up, of course ... and there was the time he'd cut his tongue. And Jane had smelled the vet. Now, he was tired. He lay down and pushed the loose plank back and forth and poked his nose into the space behind it. And when he did that, he became aware of a stronger scent ... and he held back the plank, and he saw (*This is not meant to be a surprise. E.T.*) another letter, or possibly more than one new letter, from Jane. This or these smelled to be more recent, he thought, than the others and looked to be easier to read. They were written on blue-lined paper such as students use in school.

JANE LETTER #27

Dear Danny,
So much has happened since I wrote you last.

(I was in favor of editing out the opening of this letter because it represents a terrible cliché among letter openings. I mean, if one has read even a modest series of letters, one has encountered at least one opening per every ten letters with this exact wording, either this or something like "since I last wrote you." Really. BUT, because of "our" decision about not cleaning up some previous messes, on the basis of preserving the integrity of the original, I was talked out of cleaning up this one too. I fear I have allowed a precedent to be set that will haunt me in future days. After I explained the meaning of cliché, Danny argued that he saw no need to change the wording here; he said he thought everyone needed a good cliché every now and then, that a familiar old cliché once in a while is probably a comforting sound; it probably makes us all feel closer together, as if we were all much the same underneath and" in the same basket," whatever that means. I, myself, have no need to feel the same as anyone else I meet, and what I think is that anything Jane does is all fine with Danny, come what may. So. But again, on with the letter. E.T.)

For one thing, maybe you have seen and maybe read by now (Oh, Danny, maybe you are reading at this very moment!) the letters that are there where I left the first ones you will read, and then you will be here ... or on your way here to the awing restaurant... where you will find this one! You'll see ... and smell it, too! But ... where was I? Oh, yes, the awning restaurant, the most important thing:

201

The awning restaurant closed down only a short time after I moved there. Upon looking back at the menu, I can see how that may have happened: A place that offers turnips in a brown garlic sauce as a side dish will not be appealing to the culinary tastes of many animals even if the menu says it will.

At any rate, once it had closed, a gloom settled in. Tom had well described the sort of greasy emptiness that inhabits such a place; I see it too: There is nothing more discouraging than a restaurant without anything possible to eat, with only a couple shreds of wilted brown and green lettuce, flattened and clinging to the edge of a garbage can lid.

When I left, I wandered about the neighborhood as usual.

Now ... If you are reading this letter, you will note that I brought it back for you to find at the awning restaurant anyway, but you will see that I have found another ... should I call it home? Does that presume too much? Well, within a day of coming here where I am now, I realized how truly lucky I was to find such a place as this one. I know, I know! You think that I think that every new place I find is good! Well, but you'll like this one, too. You'll find flowers in boxes hanging from porch ceilings all around the front and sides, and clean colorful stones, where humans sit and eat on metal tables. You may recognize it from your walks, or not. Now, when you get here, you'll go around to the back, where there is a sign that says, "NO LOITERING" and where you will see much the same things as you see in back of most restaurants: grease-stained cement where garbage cans have stood and overflowed and don't get washed, empty boxes, stacked with large ones on top of small ones so that they all fall over with a nudge, lots of dirty rags and brooms, storage areas, with holes in them and boards missing. This place has two wooden sheds with a platform between them where the garbage cans sit. One of these sheds has large holes in the rotten boards along its bottom back side; the other has a door space without its door in it, and even though it's open all the time, the floor is dry inside and full of boxes, too, mostly boxes of unopened cans and such, piled several dogs' height high to make hallways, much like the pantry where we lived together. Now that

I've described it, I see it is much like any back alley way, and I don't know why it would make me feel lucky.

Oh, but that's it! The best part of the place is the two human men that come out and sit on the platform steps and bring us special food—really solid meat, slabs of steak they call it, cuts that we don't usually find in the ordinary garbage, and cooked clean, often completely without sauces. Anyway, I could tell that these two humans wanted me to come closer and greet them, but I was much too nervous, at first. The second time I saw them, I was so hungry I overcame my fear—to some extent:

One of the men put what looked and smelled to be part of a hamburger down on the steps between his feet. The other man was humming some music and hitting his fingers and hands on his legs to go with the music. I sat down. I watched. I got up and went three steps closer. From there, I could see that these were not men in the same way your Master was, the man at our old home. I decided they were younger men but not as young as the boy who came to walk you now and then. Well, I sat down again, and the one with the hamburger said something like, "I know you're hungry, little cat, and I know you're afraid, but we won't hurt you." I hadn't heard any real human speech for a while, but that was the gist of it anyway. And then, the strangest thing: he opened the bread and took what was there of the burger patty out, and with a paper napkin, he carefully wiped all the sauces away and put down what was left, just the meat, on the lowest step. Well, I took that to be a strong invitation, for I didn't want the bun, of course, or the tomato, lettuce, or onion. I didn't really want the mayo, mustard, or catsup coverings either. And he knew that.

"It's hard to find the meat what with all this mess on top," he said. "And when you're a cat, smaller pieces are easier to handle, too." And with that, he began breaking the patty into pieces the size of mouse heads; I could smell those pieces stronger and stronger. "I can tell you're pretty hungry, so you don't need to stand on ceremony with us. Just come right on over here and help yourself."

Well, as you of all creatures know, Danny Lunder, sometimes there's nothing to do but to take a chance on a good outcome.

These two young men had become very still. The singing one also now sat with both hands quiet and resting flat on his legs while I ate.

There were pieces of paper napkin here and there in with the pieces of hamburger, and as they slipped into my mouth, I thought of you.

When I finished I did move a dog's length or two away to clean up.

One of the men spoke while I worked: "Are you just off on a holiday, my good cat, a little afternoon jaunt, some free time in the sun, a break from your regular home routine, or are you an animal who makes a free-wheeling, devil-may-care life on the street as a full-time beggar?" He paused to sip his drink. "Not to pry."

"You could be at least a little politically correct, Chris," the other one said. Then, he spoke to me: "You have to forgive my brother. 'Beggar' is the old fashioned word. Think 'homeless.' But even when you're out having some fun, I imagine sometimes it's a long haul from meal to meal. And a pure life on the street with that daily need for a meal will lead a body to do hard things—like taking food from strangers with nasty mouths. Like washing dishes in a restaurant even."

They both laughed and clicked their drink bottles when, almost at once, there was a call from inside. The guys spoke along with it: "Yo, Jon and Chris, get your butts in here, count of three!"

At the sound of the inside voice, so loud and harsh, I got up and backed away.

"I don't blame you for that," said the one called Chris.

"So long, little pilgrim," said the one called Jon. "Come and see us again."

And they went inside. I thought to myself that I wished they would not go inside that restaurant. The outside is better.

The next night, I checked back around the same time and found them there. Indeed, they have been coming out every night, and along with the burger patties or meat strips, they have started bringing me the dry kibbles too, the ones we used to have at the old place. They know I like the real meat better, but they leave a dish of the dry food just inside the open door in the storage shed, just in case I need a snack, and it lasts until the next night.

It is my fortune to recognize that one restaurant closing down may bring about a struggle but may also bring about a possibility: a better one nearby.

So. Here's to more and better eating establishments and humans to go with them and to whatever else you may need, wherever you may be, dear Danny. And since you are not here, I will take this letter to the Awning Restaurant as I said. If, if by some chance that place has reopened and is not safe for leaving letters, I will leave everything here underneath the far side of the small shed in the back.

      Your cat,

      Jane

JANE LETTER # 28

(Dear Reader, move ahead with caution. Let those who feel there is too much sex and violence in the arts today remember that these topics are acceptable if they are socially redeeming; we must trust that they will stir up important issues, situations the artist thinks everyone in society needs to be aware of but can only know through these specific activities. As a roach sees it, the problem is that we have to endure all the sexual and violent activities and get all the way to the end before we can tell whether we think they were socially whatever, redeeming, or not—to us. And by then, it's too late. We could have suffered for nothing. With that reminder in mind but in an effort to preserve the destitute mood and seedy atmosphere behind the scenes of the typical American restaurant, the place where Jane was driven to take lodging, we have retained most of the original language in this next letter because, as Danny reminds me, now that he is a fan of the cliché, one creature's trash is another one's treasure, and that's important too. E.T.)

Dear Danny,

If you are not here with me by the time I finish this present letter, I will take it back to leave at the awning restaurant, too… unless other events occur. And we know we mustn't be surprised when more and more other events do occur!

Shortly after I found this place, thanks to disaster, perseverance and luck and after I took up residence, thanks to wooden sheds, absent doors, rotten boards, and aisles of boxes, two other unexpected things happened. First, I noticed some little changes in my disposition and fur layout, and second, I encountered a truly unusual rodent who has, for one thing, a truly unusual past. My fur condition will be of interest to her, so I must tell you about the rodent. First of all, I admit I haven't seen all of her for more than a few seconds at a time. Hazel, as she calls herself, looks at glance like an ordinary mouse, a bit larger than average, with mouse-like ears and head, but on closer glance you see a richer, brownish yellow fur instead of the traditional gray that one expects in a mouse and, once, I saw a short, nicely swinging furless tail, which we all know is still hard to hold onto, but that's not anything to talk about now. When this Hazel eats, she sits up on her haunches and takes on an expression of intelligence that I think is also unlike the average mouse. Why sitting up to eat should set one apart to appear more intelligent, I don't know really; it's something I would not choose to do, and I consider myself to be moderately intelligent. Anyway, it seems that she is a rodent called a "gerbil," from a place called "Australia," which is some distance off in the rest of the world, not part of our locale at any rate, and she wandered away from a cage left out to catch sunlight in her backyard. Her humans had failed to fully close the door.

"I didn't know I was *in* a bloody cage until I checked out," she says. "Then, out I am, free as a bird, to coin a phrase, except sitting on a rump on the ground, just a little lost Innocent. Slowly I lifted my nose, and there it was: the scent of the outback, the call of the vast prairies, the far-flung grasslands; before I knew it, I was cavorting like a kangaroo, leaping twice my length, twisting in the air, tossing away my back legs, and then finally, at ease, finally nibbling, one after another, all the various warm grasses in front of me, following my nose, this way and that … and, in the end, lost forever."

Leaving the cage was a mixed blessing, she then tells me, what with life on the outside being unpredictable as it is. Living out in the grass, especially short-cut lawn grass, is fearful, she says, but she says, she soon had no idea how to find her way back to the cage, even if she'd wanted to. I surely have felt the same way. And speaking of mixed feeling, even though she is a gerbil and not a mouse, I find myself unable just to listen as she speaks; no, it's true; as we carry on a polite conversation, I notice I am reacting to her as if … well, I can't stop watching her whiskers move as she sits there twitching and sniffing, perhaps nibbling on a pinto bean or pasta tube. And as far as twitching goes, my tail will not stop either; the whole time we were telling our life stories, my tail was flopping about, back and forth, up and down, like a spring worm flopping on a sidewalk. I wanted to sit on it—my tail, I mean.

Out of consideration for another creature down on its luck, I want to sit on my tail when it behaves like that, so rude and instinctive. Well, Hazel doesn't seem to mind though, maybe doesn't even notice. She has a lot to talk about, a lot to say about any subject that comes up; for a small rodent and one that has been in a cage all her life, she has lots of opinions. Most of what she says applies to her own kind, but some things explain a good deal about life in general, which, I suppose, must relate to the "universal" as Maisie spoke of it. Hazel speaks about restaurants, as she does about everything else, from just inside the opening of a small crack up the steps and to the right of the main back kitchen door, and she never holds anything back; she speaks her mind entirely.

Unfortunately, her mind is hard to hear at times because her accent is a strange one. Still, I'll try to reproduce some of what she says to give you a flavor of her personality:

"I dunno why I ever set a bloomin' foot outside that bloody cage in the first place," she says. "There are some things worse than a bloody cage, old chap, and this place right where you're sittin' is one of 'em."

Other than a thing that holds someone inside it, I tried to picture what exactly her cage might look like: Is it similar to the thing you went to the vet in, for instance, which, I believe you called a "carrier"? And then there's the box the man used when he took me away from my first home, which was just called a "box," but was unlike a box just sitting around waiting to be gotten into. That being said, why was Hazel's cage bloody? Did being in it have something to do with being hurt? Maybe. So, I don't know whether a cage might be that much more hurtful than any of these other containers; maybe they're all cages. But instead of asking about that, I decide to check on what might be of more immediate import:

"This place?" I say and look around at my location. "This is a dangerous place, then, you would say? This place where I am sitting … exactly here … or the whole general area …? I haven't been here long, but I haven't seen any other than the usual dangers so far."

"Dangerous!!?? You bet yer bleedin' tail it's dangerous! Is this place dangerous? Is a bloody garage disposal dangerous? Poison everywhere you bloody well step, people with brooms behind every bloody door. You lookin' for danger around here, old bloke, you don't even have to open your eyes."

"That could be the reason I'm experiencing these strange ripples in my disposition and fur," I say, thinking indeed this could be the case. "Could that be intuitions of danger I'm feeling?"

"That or sex," says Hazel. "Bloody hormones."

Danger … sex or … hormones … none of it sounded good to me.

"Are you a female cat?"

"I believe I am," I say. "They call me 'Jane' and 'she' and 'her'."

Being a female seems to set Hazel off into a tirade of anger: "Bloody commoner Cockney trash! Setting another poor bird out to walk the streets, to walk the streets in total ignorance of their denizens, with not the first bleeding idea how to deal with sex, hormones, and the bloody dangers thereof, totally at the mercy of nature's way, bloody likely without any motherly instructions, bloody likely without any mother at all, teetering about, tra, la, la, a meal here, a bed there. And it's in a place like this you bloody well end up."

"Well. Yes," I say. "I suppose I do." I look around again to see where I am before I look up at Hazel. That uncalled-for reference to my mother doesn't sit too well with me, that and the flounder with white sauce I'd eaten for lunch, I suppose. The whole conversation was almost enough to end our bloody—I mean, budding—whatever it was, possibly friendship, right there.

"Naturally, I have a mother," I say, "A good mother too. It's just that I was taken away from her at a young age."

"Well, of course you were. Isn't that what you all were? As if that makes everything hunky doory. Well, I've seen enough of such cast-away kitten types, mate, in and out the door, wild as wallabies. And look at you; you're at the age now for hormones and sex. Take me word. And somebody bloody well better fill you in on the run of things, prepare you for the ins and outs of the inevitable."

"They don't sound so pleasant, I think." From the way she speaks I am picturing lots of blood in the course of the inevitables.

"Some pleasant, some not so bad, some worse than you could imagine, like everything else." Hazel was wiping her whiskers just like a mouse as she said this, and it was all I could do to sit still.

"Could you be so kind as to explain these things to me then? I suppose I'd better find out the worst sooner than later because no matter how bad it is, if it's going to happen, one is better off expecting it than not. I guess I could use an extra mother."

"A second Mum, then. That's me all right. Here. Have a seat. Take a listen. For one thing, it's all leadin' in the end to a pile of furry bundles of bloody little miniature replicas of yourself, and they'll be wandering aimlessly all over your sorry body, or, in my case, we see fur-less little fetus-looking things squeaking around *under* me belly."

"Oh," I exclaim, feeling much relieved and on safer ground, "kittens you mean! I was told about these by an old cat I knew once in … well, in a place I lived once …" All my words were falling into each other and crashing to a stop: I was feeling how it was to be with Maisie, and you, Danny, and my heart filled like a balloon, to crowd everything else out. I almost stopped listening.

"Kittens. That's right, me girl, three or four, up to six, maybe even seven of the little buggers. You'll feel pushed and pulled and shoveled around much as bacon on a griddle."

After a minute I could breathe and swallow, accept being where I am now, a place by the garbage cans in back of another restaurant. "As I remember … as I remember, this cat who first told me about kittens didn't care for the experience."

"Well, knock a koala bear off a *Eucalyptus* branch, as they say. Never mind. According to me good instincts, you're gonna shine as a bloody Mum. Mumhood's gonna come to you natural as eatin' a mouse. Oh, sorry about that. Never mind. All right. I'm fixin' to fill you in on the whole circumstances."

"That'll be helpful ... I hope," I said, and I was hoping the worst was over, hoping to bypass the koala bears, whatever they might be.

"First of all, you got to find yerself a bloody mate, mate." She laughs loud and hearty at this remark, and I chuckled too, although, I promise you, I do not know what she finds so funny. Maybe it's an old Australian expression we aren't familiar with. "Then," she says, "Then, comes the crashing, fearful excitement of the-"

> (*Danny and I agreed to edit out the brief section of this letter in which Hazel describes the sexual act because, although it may be accurate to the experience of gerbil sex, according to our research, it does not reflect the feline sexual encounter enough to be useful. For that reason, we skipped to the end of this description. We do, however, entertain the possibility of providing more complete information in an appendix. E.T.*)

"Then in a while ... I don't seem to remember the exact time lapse, but one day, there they are, the little ones, here they come, sliding out, one at a time, all naked and slippery—exact little replicas of you, yourself, waiting for you to clean 'em up and show 'em what's what."

> (*Jane explains later in a portion of a letter we deleted that Hazel's account of the gerbil birth and family life was a good deal different from what Jane experienced with a cat birth. The kittens were not all carbon copies of Jane, for one thing, and for another, the behavior of the father was in no way like that of Hazel's mate. But more on that subject in a section we did not delete. E.T.*)

"I see," I say, although I am far from seeing most of what Hazel says (and why do we so often say we see when we don't; I was experiencing a fit of pique). Nevertheless, I pushed ahead: "What do you "show" them when you show them what's what?"

"What to eat, for one thing, girlie."

"Oh. What to eat. I do see."

"Right here. You see." And she pointed to the little bumps on her stomach. "Nothing to it! They'll just bloody well suck everything out of your belly bumps there, happy as can be."

"I see." This time, I look down and remember cleaning these bumps.

"There's a bit of discomfort as they make their ways out, you know. They have to leave through a tunnel that's a tight squeeze for 'em if you know what I mean. It's a closed in, sort of a ... well, it's a bloody narrow sort of a ... well, I don't know what it's bloomin' like inside, do I? Never mind. The location will become clear to you along the way."

"Along the way."

"And all along the way, yer ever-lovin' mate is bringing you food and is also bringing back any of the little ones that wander away or roll off the edge of the nest. Did I mention they will all be blind?"

I could not think of a single word to say. As you can imagine, Danny, this information was more than I wanted to take in all at once. I just wanted her to be still. But she went on and on about those babies, and it's the only time I'd heard her speak for so long without becoming "bloody" angry. Even when they mysteriously disappeared one day, she seemed agreeable; she seemed happy because a new batch was on the way. Until they removed her mate from the cage. But she claims she never missed the old ones. You can bet that sent me a sharp jolt. What if all mothers felt the same, if my mother did when Boots and I were taken away?

And yet, I think I'll put that question aside for now. When you're already in a seriously precarious position, not knowing anything for sure about your future, and you begin to hear of unsettling new possibilities, possibilities of things you'd never ever considered before because you'd never exactly ever heard of them before even though they now sound to be a definite part of your future, well, that's not the time to try to answer some indefinite, biological question from your past. You'll only feel more desolate. Still, I will say that Hazel's descriptions of sex and hormones made me think she'd had lots of experience with both.

Hazel's motherly talk went on, or off and on, for three days at least, and then ... and then, just as if it had all been planned out, CS arrived.

> (*I find myself apologizing again to all readers: Jane's record of Hazel's seemingly endless tirade on the subject of the birds and bees leaves me grinding my mandibles. Well, I don't have teeth, do I? I'm trying to remember how Danny persuaded me not to remove some of it, but then, I think, my explanation might have grown just as tedious as the Gerbil's, mighten it?.*
>
> *Never mind.*

There is an abrupt end to this letter, and, at first, Danny was afraid something awful had happened to Jane to cause her to stop writing like that. He was so agitated he began to pant and paw at the pages until he ruined two of them before he found the middle of the next letter. We will never know what, if any, crucial plot evolvements may have been lost in those soggy, churned up pages, and we are reminded again that, as genres go, the memoir is subject to various kinds of assaults: benign, malicious, and accidental. So be it.

Then, on top of all that literal mess, Danny and I built a mountain out of a mole hill arguing whether to number this segment as a new letter or to attach it to the one above. But here's what it says: E.T.)

hard for me to find time to write. He was from the beginning a most attractive young cat, all bright orange and clean white—in fact, looking much like old Tom but shiny and lively and obviously so taken with me that he hung around for days being helpful and funny before I succumbed to his charms. One can't be too careful in this world, as Hazel says. Hazel, by the way, is keeping out of sight much of the time now.

But to go on: When he first arrived, led by his proud white chest and prancing as if he had pop bugs attached to his feet, he was extremely hungry and might also have been tired. Well, our friends Jon and Chris hadn't yet come out with the good meal of the day, so CS helped himself to some coleslaw left over from lunch. At this time, Hazel was watching from her crack beside the door.

Now, Hazel frequently eats coleslaw and lettuce, things like that; she's pretty much a vegetarian. It doesn't bother me, but I was amazed to see how vigorously the new orange cat licked up that sauce and chewed down shreds of cabbage, murring with delight. Because he enjoyed it so much, we thought to call him CS .

"Keep an eye on that one," said Hazel, "a slaw-eating cat could be trouble."

"I eat most anything creamy these days," CS said as he chewed; "I eat lots."

"He's got worms," Hazel said.

I admit he talked as he chewed, and the cabbage spilled from his mouth, but sometimes one has to overlook small faults in a new friend. Did I say he was funny? He'd go running halfway up the garbage can enclosure, look all around as if he'd forgotten how he got there, then jump down and hop around, here and there, like the walkway was a hot grill and he had to run up the wall again so as not to get fried feet!

When I begin to feel drawn to CS's company, Hazel, who, as I said, is staying mostly inside the door crack, was, nevertheless, encouraging: She says not to worry even while she advises caution, and now I think of it, as a rodent, how could Hazel ever be entirely at ease with CS? Well, and I know she wanted me to keep an open mind about him, too. But I also know, despite my short life, that it takes a while to undo a knot of fear even when there's a pull of attraction. And the combination can make you dizzy.

So, even though I was hesitant at first, it turns out that CS and I have a lot in common, similar backgrounds for one thing, both having been abandoned at an early age. Now, Danny Lunder, you know most of my life events, but CS and I had to tell each other about ours, so one early morning as we strolled in and around the metal restaurant chairs and tables, with all the flowers above and their sweet scents falling on our noses below, I tell CS about you and me and our old times and encourage him to tell me about his own old times.

"I was born somewhere, about five months ago," he informs me; "Not too far along afterwards, I was cold; I was hungry. Everyone was crying; then everyone slept a week or more, and I left, and I don't want to talk about it. Spent days, the whole winter, trying to keep warm, went under an oil heater, back of the Seven Eleven, kept hiding from some dogs I ran into, controlled the water ditch. Behind the tire store. And eating everything I could find. You know that Chinese place with the fish pond outside? I can tell you: in cold water, those fish slow down to a barely drifting speed. Pretty white

215

and orange things, sort of like me. But worry, worry, worry… always worrying: What if I missed a fish, lost balance and fell in the pond? Cold? 'Eyaha!' Other things like that."

Of course, I tell him then about falling off the rim into the water shower tub and what I worry about now, too, but, the way things go, we two, we just figure we can't be sure we will be safe; we just have to go on hoping for good luck like everybody else.

And that very afternoon some time before supper, when I have only known him, maybe, two weeks, CS asks me to come along with him to a special place he knows of for a special treat he can find there; this is how he words it: "I'll show you something will spin you out of your pretty gray head."

Well, what sort of thing is that to say to someone you hardly know? I want to ask a question back this time: Why would anyone want to spin out of her head anyway? I look over at Hazel.

" Don't even put your *tongue* out near a mushroom," she says; then, she just wiggles her nose and backs her way into the darkness of her home.

So, before I know what's happening, off we go, CS and I, and, as destiny would have it, we need to cross over the Dead Street, the wide street filled with cars, both moving and standing, the same street where Jake had been killed. When we arrive at the curb, I begin to tell CS about Jake, and he listens hard, but I can tell he has little sympathy in his heart for the story.

"I don't hold no truck in animals with slimy tails," he says. "Can't trust 'em."

"Why not?"

"Don't know, I just know it's true. So did my mom."

"What if they lead you to food?"

"Well, that's another thing, I guess. I guess I could think about that."

"Do you think they would take your food?"

"Maybe."

"Well, what about me? I eat the same as you."

"You're a female. That's different."

"Different how?" I am intrigued now by this whole topic.

"For one thing, I know I can mess you up if I have to, no problem."

"Oh."

"For another thing ..." He stops and looks around as if to catch his bearings. "Maybe I just don't feel like talking about it anymore."

As you can tell, CS is one of those who favor action before words. We travel on a while, and we come to a little bricked-in space, full of plants—plants in the ground, plants in pots, even one plant coming out of, what looked to be, a stone rabbit; the area is small, no more than the size of 10 or 12 garbage cans pushed together, but it is thick with green growing things and colorful flowering things—all opening up to the recent warm air and their new spring lives.

"What a wonderful time my nose is having," I say, winding happily through the greenery.

"You'll hook your nose up to your whole body when you take a bite of this leaf I'm showing you," says CS, and he removes a leaf from about head high on a scraggily looking bush by the wall, and he carefully chews it up. Next, he does the strangest thing: he pushes down to the ground one entire branch or stalk of that plant, clawing its leaves as it sinks down; then he throws himself onto the stalk, rolling and twisting back and forth, butting his head against the stem and leaves, purring in what seems to be a state of rapture.

"Whoopee! Try it! Come on! Be a sport," he calls. "Let yourself go! It won't hurt you. I promise."

For a minute I think I hear angry words, the sort of words Hazel uses, coming from behind the wall—lots of "bloodies" and "buggers" and "blimies."

I'm just not sure what to do.

Pretty soon, I see that CS has stopped thrashing about and is lying on his back, completely at his ease and quiet. He seems to have a sort of smile on his face. I think he looks so friendly lying there.

I take a small bite of a small leaf and chew it slowly as CS did. The taste is not unpleasant. I take a few more. I sniff at the plant and lie down on the stalk that CS had crushed. I roll over on it. I don't feel anything like a whoopee, though I do feel sleepy.

"Everybody's different," I think to myself. Who knows how something will affect someone else or even herself. Hadn't I thought that thought before, just recently? Well. It bears rethinking, I guess. I wonder if you have heard about such a plant, Danny?

After a while in which nothing more happened, CS and I make our way back across the Dead Street and behind the restaurant. We are just in time for the late night garbage dump. That evening, I can tell you exactly, the thrown-out garbage meal is mostly some kind of rice that looks dirty and lots of vegetables on long stalks, a few odd rolls, of course, and large portions of lettuce and such. A few pats of butter are all I feel like eating at that point myself. I think I'll wait for Jon and Chris to bring out their special meat of the day. CS is afraid of the humans, so he stays out of sight, but that night, I am so glad to see those guys that I go right up as they sit down, and I do a double leg rub, across all four of their legs, pressing up and down, and they stroke my back, both ways too, head to tail, tail to head, ending with a nice face rub: along the mouth, over the eyes and between the ears. It feels wonderful to me.

Jon says I purr as loud as a coffee machine; Chris says more like a tractor. They give me pieces of Delmonico Steak. They ask if I want it rare or medium. They laugh and keep on rubbing me as I eat. New, close human friends add a loving dimension to the restaurant life, at least in my opinion they do.

Much later, when everything is closed up, CS comes out and consumes over his weight in rice and cold steak. Afterwards, we wash each other's faces and play in and around the boxes in the open-door shed. And so there develops yet another dimension to restaurant life, one of my own kind.

Oh, Danny Lunder, I am hoping you will be here soon, with plans to stay and see how all these things turn out. I will leave my letters and good wishes over at the Awning restaurant, or else, here, under the small shed ... to wait until you arrive and find them.

Jane

JANE LETTER #29

Dear Danny,

More news to let you know how things are: Soon after CS and I had "taken up together" as she said, Hazel decided to move much farther back into the restaurant walls; she claimed she could get fresher and faster and more of her preferred food back there, farther back inside. I think, however, for her, it was a matter of keeping an eye on one cat who lived in an area of limited food access compared with keeping an eye on two when one of them turned out to be livelier than a Garter snake and rummaged around in more places than she could keep track of. It must have seemed to her that our space out back here would soon hold too many cats to be numbered. I still see her once in a while, and I warn her to watch what she eats and to avoid little food-filled cages and pads. But she knows all that. She was the one to warn me of such dangers.

And not long after Hazel moved back inside, CS moved on as well. Unlike Hazel's mate, CS claimed he couldn't settle down to stay in a nest, that he had to travel on down the road, that he felt a strong power vibrating along his tail, something he couldn't really describe, and he couldn't sit still for long. Well, it's true that CS never exhibited an introspective side to his nature, so maybe, as I said, he was primarily a physical being. "He's a male cat," Hazel said later. She spoke as if his sex and species told everything about him although, as I think things over, I don't know how Hazel got so much cat information, since she lived mostly in a cage with another gerbil. On one of the occasions when we met again, I asked her about her knowledge and opinions, and sure enough, as I might have expected, she explained that her cage had been in the large kitchen of a large house where she had lived, in the center of life, with parents and children, dogs, snakes, lizards, fish, and even a

219

rabbit for a brief period—with all sorts of creatures, in and out, off and on. She surveyed a small cosmos, herself in the middle. She is definitely worldly wise; on the other hand, I don't remember her mentioning a cat.

As for CS, I think maybe he never did feel safe here either, with the humans around. And how could he? He'd had no opportunity to experience the human touch the way I had. Well, of course, everything comes and goes, or in this case, goes. Except for Double00, who has discovered my nightly extra food supply and shows up regularly at the invisible door of the larger shed. I stay out of his way entirely now.

I lie high up on boxes; I wait for you and the babies.

Waiting again, but full of love in more ways than one!

Jane

JANE LETTER #30

Dear Danny,

You'll never believe! Such an unexpected surprise came about! One morning soon after I last wrote, I eased my head around the frame of the perpetually open shed door to find, of all cats, Maisie! She was licking up some kind of clear sticky-like fluid, something that I could see sliding down one side of the green plastic garbage can and ending up on her tongue.

" Maisie! Is that you?" To see her, as I said, was a surprise to me!

She turned and looked and moved closer to the shed. "Are you a cat? What cat? Speak up, dahling, or I shall have to wipe your eyes out."

So it was Maisie, all right, and her cataracts had gotten worse, of course, and much of her looked very different from what we remember. She looked a mess, to be truthful; her hair, where it still grew, was lumpy with mats; even worse were the places where it was gone, her ears and lower neck, now hair free, showed blotchy red bumps dripping a yellowish fluid. Well, I am beginning to learn about fleas myself, and I noticed we both were scratching a good bit as we talked.

"Just take a look at you; it's our little Lady Jane," and she did just that, her eyes up close to my belly. "So round and full of the fruits of life, of the life on the streets!"

"I guess I am," I said, as usual not knowing how to respond to Maisie, one who had never even stepped, much less let herself fall, into the category of friend.

"And still showing that disorganized, splotchy gray coat, I see." She began to bite and furiously pull at the hair between the toes of her left hind foot.

"And you still wearing your long ..." and I couldn't think of any honest other thing to say, "long ... hair."

"One's hair can be an asset one minute, you know, and a liability the next, just like everything else, you know. This toe hair... filling in between the pads... nice and warm in January, then in March, when I am taking a leap onto some unknown window sill, dahling, what a loooong forward, then downward slide! Hair-covered foot pads allow no stopping grip at all. On a slippery surface, you go right over the edge."

"I never thought of that."

"Well, shorthairs never have to."

"No. But I have had dangers to confront."

"Ummm." She was chewing away at that foot.

"What happened to you then after the man put me out ...? And Danny ... Do you have any news of Danny Lunder?"

"I hate to say it, my dear, but when you were first gone, I would enter each room like a queen on her red carpet. You know how I'd always hissed at you—at the way you raced around the house and stopped behind doors, the way she looked at you all soppy eyed... and, of course, at the food you ate ...

"I know."

"Well, I'm working through those issues as we speak: group work. Oh, my dear, I'm beginning to see what expansive bowls of emptiness caused my little inner kitten so many negative feelings, so many resentments; I'm reconnecting to that little kitten inside, to her life, all boxed up in a house within a house, all bound up by rules for everything, sitting alone in a cage, never knowing the wild abandonment, the unstructured frolicking, the joy of a simple romp in a trash pile. The poor little beauty grew up as a plaything, a mere toy.

"Yes, delving into the past, I have seen how the Cat Show Circuit made me sick somewhere down deep inside ... although I admit it did give my early life a focus, you know, a direction, a thing so lacking in the lives of our young today."

"But you never seemed to be lacking in the self-esteem that they talk about so much today." I said this because it was true.

"Ah, the faux self-esteem," she said. "Yes, my little dear, the self-esteem that is built on plastic trophies, on tacking up a few long-ago-faded blue ribbons."

"Well, I never thought of it that way."

"And so, when it all ended, the emptiness filled my little kitten up with a hunger for real meaning."

"And maybe for the food I had been getting," I thought.

"When the new woman came to take me with her, I was nothing but skin and bones in a fur coat. It's true. Well, my dear, she fed me all right for a few days. And then one morning, in the middle of a normal trip to the grooming parlor, she had me shaved. She had my entire body shaved of its luscious hair. To remove the mats. Can you picture what I saw in the mirror that night? And to think, she quite unsuspected, having never seen it, my fury; she gasped in surprise when I left between her legs as she took in the newspaper the next morning."

I tried to picture Maisie in a place I'd never seen, without her hair, in a sense, naked, but I could only see the past. "I can only see us in the house with the Christmas tree and the way we looked then." Maisie was staring at the past also, I think; I couldn't tell for sure, due to the hazy white film of the cataracts. "But you do know what happened to Danny," I began. "When did you see him at the end?"

"My last awareness of that yellow dog was the sound of the indomitable, optimistic tail thumping against the porch railing just before one of his walks. He was shut in the basement when the woman picked me up."

"He always did look on the bright side of things."

"Sweetie, to the point of injuring himself at times."

Not wanting to get into a scrap with Maisie, I changed the subject.

"Would you want to stay here around this restaurant, then? It's fairly quiet, and there are two good humans who bring regular food."

"Well, my dear, I did go through a brief restaurant phase when I was first out free. I'm finished with all that now." She looked at me with one ear laid back. "No, no, no. No more restaurants for me, dahling. You may not believe it but waitresses, even truck drivers, still try to grab hold of me. Never a minute's peace. Just another drawback to having long hair, I suppose, of being so beautiful. I want to put all that away; today I am basking in the sun of the most authentic poetical material I ever experienced; I'm just soaking up all these real-life, street-dramas, you know: Oh, the minor irritations of insect bites to the major pains of ageing, starvation, disease, disappointment, failure, loneliness and loss ... Did I say starvation? All of that, Muse to my art."

"And to think I never saw this ... this "opening up" side of you, Maisie. Well, maybe once in a while, the times you chased me up and down the stairs, that time you trapped me under the rug in the bathroom."

"We had moments; I remember." She blinked and tried to look at me. "I suppose I'll be heading off now. Listen, lady girl, I'm connected with a group down by the hospital; the food there comes regularly, too and nobody tries to get near you. If you ever need a rest ... It's a sort of cat commune, and all the males have been "taken care of" as they say, well females, too, but that goes without saying, always the females.

"Now, I'm going to leave you with a poem to remember me by. I know how you liked my work; I know how you even committed some of it to memory."

"I did. I still say it."

"All right then, you may have this one:

SHEETS OF PAVEMENT, STRIPS OF LIFE

I salute myself!
And every creature outside of me.
Every creature upon me
The tiny ear mite, his rustling song,
The mosquito's shrill whistle
I will listen to hear and look to see
I will step easy along the street

Around those who lie waiting
Over those who're asleep.
They are every part of me, whom I know and whom do not.
We have leapt from high places and landed on our feet.
We have lived on the road strong of heart
We will greet each other the same.
All in one, we live apart!

I sit quietly at the end. This poem is different from the others. Maisie has done some hard learning from her life on the street, as we all have.

"I can tell this poem has spoken to you," she says. "And now, this time I will go, but good luck to you and to the ones that will come from you. May we meet again someday, if not the very next one."

She bumped into side of the building, head on, but then her head, followed by the rest of her, disappeared in front of that flowing, still wavy tail, as she left.

"But wait," I called. "What is a hospital? And where is it located?"

She was gone. I thought about her tail, and then yours, Danny, both gone.

Other friends lost.

And you are not here yet.

So it is that I am alone again as my belly swells up. Mostly, I rest, thinking of past circumstances: bushes, porches, sheds, soft beds and hard. Well, at least this time I know what to expect. In some way! And for now, the days fall out the same: the same sounds, the same scents, discards and leftovers from the same menu, day after day, but then the same warm hands and treats from the humans also, and I think some things are best left the same.

Tonight, I can feel the little ones turning around inside like a family of newts settling under a log for the night. There must be a lot of them. How many did Hazel project? Sometimes I feel uncertain, but right now I feel sleepy, slow and sleepy ...

Wherever you are, may your sleep be warm and slow, dear Danny Lunder.

Jane

JANE LETTER #31

Dear Danny,

I am writing in new sorrow on some notebook paper left here by one of the humans, Chris or the one called Jon, who must be gone now along with everything else, along with all that was here only a few days ago. And how foolish, even for a moment, to think of anything remaining the same.

Here is what happened: The very night I finished the last letter to you, at about the usual time and before I grew sleepy, Chris and Jon arrived on schedule with their special food and attention. They saw me waiting inside the larger shed door and called out: "Come here, little Gray Lady; come here and eat your fill and put on even a little more extra weight where you need it."

"There you are, little mama to be, little pudgy, potbellied gal."

"We have a taxi waiting to escort you to your new lodgings in the country -"

"Shhhh!" The one pulls the hat down over the other's eyes and looks at me. "Come on over here, you not-so-little Gray Lady. We brought you some special canned food, something you can't resist: cat tuna ... in oil ... Yum, yum, yum ... and also, on the side, this cozy little box. Look at this blanket in here ... warm and safe ..."

I was so glad to see them I was only half hearing their words or anything else closely—torn between rubbing against their legs and eating what food they put down on the steps, eating too fast, of course.

"Hold on, there. Take it easy, easy, girl."

"There's lots more where that came from. Here you go."

"Slow down now."

And they stroked and scratched my back and I ate and purred and I felt their hands.

"We need to … slowly … pick you up, Lady Gray …"

"Let's see … how we can do this …?"

"If we try … to … carefully … lift…"

When the hands curved around me and my belly, I squiggled away quickly, automatically. I watched the box from a distance of about 13 dogs away.

"I guess not," one of the humans said.

"Not today, not yet," the other said. "Um." They stood for a few moments.

"I'm not going to miss this place."

"Yeah. We should've paid more close attention to the sign."

"Yeah. I like the sign."

"We'll think of something for our Gray Lady. Maybe a regular trap…"

"I can't believe she'd like that kind of something …"

After another moment or two, I moved away and began my clean-up.

"All right, Lady Gray cat, we'll have to figure out another strategy for rounding you up. Meanwhile, we'll leave enough food for a day or so, to keep you going. Okay?"

"I think we shouldn't leave much food. I think she needs to be extra motivated … if you know what I mean."

"Yeah. Maybe you're right."

They talked together a while more, but I stopped looking at them or paying attention. They put some dry food in the usual place just inside the open door of the larger shed where I normally sleep. As they left, I remember I called a soft cry, hoping they would come back; then, I listened to the quiet of being alone; I finished my toes and settled in for the night.

There you have the first part of the night; now, here's what happened after Chris and Jon left: I slept in my usual place on a box of canned tomatoes near the middle of the large shed. Double00 came for his meal by the door some time around mid-night or early morning. As it turned out, I found later that he finished the kibble the humans had left.

All was quiet again, the same as usual, until I awoke to the sound that means a backing truck. The sun had been up for, oh, maybe two hours human time. When I looked out, I saw a man working with a broom, trying to prop open the restaurant's back door. Three other men holding paper cups, most likely of coffee, sat and watched on the steps. One stuck his hand out and poked the man's broom:

"Broomhilda Honey, how 'bout me and you doing a little sweeping out in the back room, kill some time?"

The Broom man replied, slightly out of breath: "I'll give you time you can kill on another job, Romeo, you don't keep your hands to yourself."

I'd never seen this particular truck before; the humans lowered its back end down and went in the restaurant; they came out, one after the other, laughing and carrying things, chairs and tables, some large metal objects. All morning, instead of taking anything out of the truck, they carried things into it. No need to wonder how fearful I felt, Danny; you'll know that for sure, and you'll surely guess that, in the midst of so much fear, my thoughts flipped about like your agitated tail used to, and at that point I couldn't get a clear hold on any one thought; all I could do was to wonder what to do: to leave or hide or how or where. Then, in all that motion, I remembered a flapping loose board along the bottom edge at the far side of the smaller shed; this shed did have a door and its door was always properly locked, but, of course, there was no need for me to go *in* the shed, only under. At about noon time, when the restaurant was usually full of life, delicious with odors, the four men left and I took the chance to investigate the space around the sheds. Sure enough, I found the loose board and saw that I could push it aside, an action that seemed familiar to me. I could push my way into a sort of crawl space under the floor boards themselves. The men returned, so I stayed there all the rest of the day, the noises becoming almost a soothing hum until something would drop with a crash and someone would complain loudly. Then, close to day's end, I could hear and feel movement next door, in the larger shed, and later, over top of me in the small shed and so close that I trembled, and I couldn't tell the shaking of the floorboards from the shaking of my trembling body or that from the jiggling of the little ones settling to bed in my belly, but I knew I had no place else to go, could not trust myself to leave. No. No. Best to be quiet and do all this trembling in one place, the same place. To stay here. To tremble here.

I watched the sun shadows grow long and darker; I heard my shed door slam, the lock click, some slow talking that moved away, a laugh here and there; I heard the truck door shut and the engine start, and the backing sound again. There it was, from morning to night, and the closing sounds of that day gradually softened against the buildings, and dispersed into the waiting dusk, so assuring quietness and sleep, everything still, everything resting.

Later: At dawn, looking for water, sensing the heat of the day to come, I leave the shed crawl space, thinking of you, Danny Lunder. Do you remember how you used to take a paw and roll me back into your chest when I tried to go to the kitchen in the mornings? As I walk beside the restaurant, slowly, around to the front, I find the kind of emptiness you feel inside even before you see what's actually gone, emptiness that hangs around in the presence of unwanted things. Awnings on their sides hanging down halfway into the flower planters, planters whose flowers, I now notice, are drooping limp into their soil, and farther, around back, where I spent most of my days, garbage cans sagging with discouragement, overfilled and lopsided, with their tops half off and dreadful odors crawling out. I sit, just as discouraged, on the steps. A little morning wind cools the tuffs of my ears. The sports section of a newspaper that might have been important to read a day or so ago lifts and falls; two Miller Lite cans roll up to the steps and then down, partners in a slow, wavy dance that the same cool wind stirs up, and above them, the "No Loitering" sign joins in with a sort of blues-like accompaniment, grinding back and forth.

I don't sit for long in the middle of that sadness; I go into the large, open-door shed, looking for what, I don't know. The first thing I see, of course, on its side, is the very empty food dish that Jon and Chris have left. Not a good omen for the future. Most of the boxes remaining appear to be empty, too; they're turned over or piled up on one another in unstable positions and in no special order I can tell. At a loss, I try a jump to the top of one column just to see what's there, or just to see if I can: nothing; I jump to the next pile which falls scattered all over itself under my not-so-light-weight self. Finally I do sit again, and for some time, just outside the door, feeling completely alone and deserted. There's no doubt I'm hoping to see Hazel, no doubt I'm hoping maybe Chris and Jon will come early today, no doubt I'm remembering conversations, treats and stroking and times when things were better. And then, as it grows dark, sure enough, I hear a scratching, scratching sound from somewhere inside the walls, from inside that crack near the door.

I cry out loud and fast, "Hazel! Is that you, Hazel?" And I admit have I placed my nose right up against the opening so that the words come out "Satuazl." This is not the best way for a cat to greet a gerbil. I know that.

"Of course, it's me. Who'd ya think it'd be, a Crocodile Hunter? Back bloody up, old girl, so I can get me a look … What's going on around here?"

"That's just the trouble. Nothing is. Everything's gone."

"Well, smash me corn and millet."

"We may have to find another place."

"*You* may have to do, mate, but if you could see the stray seeds and beans lying around the walls and crevices back inside, you'd know there's enough food in this place to last me me entire gerbil life to its complete and final end, give or take a day or two."

"But you can't be sure; I can't believe you could be so sure that there's-"

"We gerbils don't live near as long as you cats do, you know, even under the best of circumstances."

"That food could be stale, it could be full of … bugs, or-"

"There's a whole tin of something called "Grits" that someone's dumped under the sink in here. It's a corn product. That pile alone will last me a year. And a year's about the time frame we're lookin' at overall, give or take a few." She laughs.

"I wish you wouldn't talk that way. I wish you'd come live out here and live with me now and tell me what to do. Give advice and talk funny all the time. I feel so heavy and pulled apart inside."

"Bloody well true, old gal. From the looks of you, it's only a matter of hours, and you're gonna feel all dumped out and empty inside and pulled apart outside."

"And I'm hungry all the time it seems like." I say that, and suddenly, without any control, my tail gives a violent twitch, big and wide, and I know Hazel has seen it. I know because, as I look back around, she is gone, all except her nose and mouth.

"Well, 'course you are," Hazel's words come out of her moving nose and mouth; "you're eating for six. Or more. Maybe I could bring you a few grains of rice and a few dried beans or so. Good source of protein that."

"I'm afraid I eat a lot more than you do, a *lot* more than you do, and I only want to eat … I only want … to eat …" I can't say the word and turn away in shame just in time to catch my tail waving on the loose again, thrashing away worse than ever.

And so Hazel disappears from sight, a shadow folding back inside the door-crack passageway, but I can hear her as she leaves: "Don't worry. You'll be bully. Just take deep breaths and count backwards. Close your eyes and think of the Queen or Mel Gibson."

Only minutes after Hazel has left, I realize that the hunger and pulling I have begun to feel inside might indicate more than just the moving of restless kittens; it might indicate a move on the part of kittens to escape my belly altogether, to find their way out into the world. And something right there told me I needed to go make that place under the locked shed into a home for the little ones, a safe place for them to enter into, or onto, or upon, when they arrived outside of me. So, I crawled back underneath the shed; my thinking is that since no one had found or bothered me yesterday, the place could be safe, safe enough for me and the babies for now.

I would have liked to have found a box for bracing against or even a gentle bowl-shaped scoop in the dirt, but nevertheless, I lay down calmly and stretched out peacefully where I waited, opening and closing my claws, purring for comfort, feeling the pulls within my belly. And, just as Hazel had said, over the some hours, one by one, four little sacks of wet babies slid out, plop, plop, plop, plop, and each one had to be licked dry and everything around it cleaned up.

A line of four. At first I couldn't tell them apart as they lay rat gray and damp in the dim under-floor light, but pretty soon I had licked them until their colors surfaced like magic paints; I checked their little feet and ears, noses and tails, over and over again. I thought of you, Danny Lunder, over and over, too, of your strong licking care. And as I settled us all to bed, I remembered hearing, during the middle of the birthing, I remembered hearing my humans calling me, "Lady Gray, Lady Gray," but of course I couldn't go out to them then, and I heard little else that night, only the babies' comforting little sucking murmurs and constant purring, those steady family sounds. (How could anyone of her own normal will pull away from them?) And thinking of pulling away, now I think of it, at some time that night, in a doze, I heard what must have been the sound of Double00 eating the food pellets that Jon and Chris surely had left for me next door, and I wished in a daze that he and all raccoons could live a long way from here...

While it was dark, I dreamed of warm fur, nests of babies and you, Danny Lunder, of how thoroughly you will lick these babies when you meet them, and how they will cup your nose and try to nip it; how they will climb your soft ears to the top and fall back. And I, I will buff your head side to side, too, and then rest between your paws.

Jane

JANE LETTER # 32

(*In another effort to convey the lively excitement of the original document, Danny and I have tried again to reproduce the exact lettering of this next note. E.T.*)

Dear Danny,
All   and
          the baabies are   over mmme.   Their   eyess
came open
yesterday and   to   day   I can see that
see
                    Maisie   was righttt about   movement. Never
                    a minute's peace. So   me   times
III have ttto llleave the
          area   to groom myself. I don'ttt mind
it,
they
thoughhh. I love to see them, whatever   do, even ttthe little
orange one
                              whoisss an   exaccct   co
               py
of CS.   wild   I call him Rochefort   All have names
ffffrom the old
from the menu.
menu and in memory of the old restaurant all names start with the
human letter R.   Never   m   ind;
you will notice   more and more   now
thattt.
I am not entirely sure how to say the names but I do like the
looooook of them. Roulade is

kind heart

gray like me   and soft   alssssso

creamy cloud patches

falling soft   under her eyes

like little souls drifting by

tTThen you will see   Rotisserie, of solid gray

hair,   longer than   and d thick   more than rest ooooof

between toes !   brighjt   green eyes

fiannalyyy there is Rueben   who is bl bl black

and   robust

easy tttto please

eager for meals,   a most regular eater

OURe humans   our good humnans still leave me   of

good food

all in goo d health

And so   we continue always,   and wait always,   always wait for

you.

Jane

JANE LETTER #33

Dear Danny,

Today is only four days after the Opening Eye day, and let me tell you, without a doubt, there are all kinds of things to say about having babies, but the main one I can think of now (and one thing is not having much time to think!) is something that both Maisie and Hazel said: When they are all safe inside you, you don't have nearly the turmoil of feelings and fears that you do once they are out and separate to themselves. Then ... then, you see each one whole, that's true, in what looks at first to be a sturdy, functional body, but when you wash them up after they eat, for instance, you can't help but notice those delicate, unfinished extremities—the soft, unused foot pads, the harmless, translucent claws and tough but tiny pink tongues ... Even in combination with one another, you know how useless these tender body parts are, and so you know each day and the next, what close attention you have to pay to keep all of you safe.

I have sensed a seventh sense, a "what can go wrong" sense.

As a mother, at first, I didn't let the babies out of sight; I stayed very close; well, they wanted to eat all the time anyway; at least I knew I had food for them. That was one thing not to worry about, and yet just when I was feeling calm in that security, there came three days when I found nothing in the bowl, when Double00 must have eaten all the food my humans had left out—either that, or else ... some other... bad thing ... I thought of possibilities: "Maybe my humans have stopped bringing the food. They might be thinking I myself have left this place along with everyone else; I haven't seen them for ... I don't know how long it's been. How long has it been? Maybe they have given up bringing food to a creature they never see."

Well, it wasn't long though before I realized I can't feed the babies enough unless I eat enough. But I did have lots of previous experience, so I figured finding food wouldn't be too hard; the neighborhood's the same, the same as it's always been ... Oh! ... I saw the trouble! It's that nothing with *me* is the same! Now I feel hesitant about going off on long, unpredictable nightly scavenges, along dark fronts of restaurant after restaurant, climbing can after can, waiting and watching for danger as I used to do; now I want to stay within ears' hearing of the nest ... I worry about something dark and cloudy becoming a solid fright, an owl, a weasel, just outside the shed, and what if the kittens cry out, needing help, and I'm not there ...

I suppose it's time to take Tom's Insect Advice more seriously. As I have written earlier, Danny, I have eaten a bug or two now and then, but without good digestion, and we've all played around with a few poppers and rollers here and there, stretching out a wide claw to prevent them from going under a rug, batting at some that flew nearby in the air, but I'd hardly given them a chance as an actual meal. I am considering the possibility there might be soft insects crawling around somewhere, insects without shell coverings, maybe even some without hairy feet ... Maybe I could bite off the feet.

(*I continue to be irritated by Jane's dismissive attitude toward insects; it's bad enough that she would consider eating some of us, but it's adding insult to injury when she allows she would only do so under great duress. E.T.*)

Later:

Nothing substantial has resulted from my trying the insect meals, nothing filling, nothing but flopping stomach movements and noises much like you make, Danny, just as some uncommon or unknown body approaches the house and while you are deciding if you will need to actually bark. In the meantime, I manage to find some garbage meals here and there, and I'm almost able to touch a fin on top of one fat-bellied Chinese fish.

While I've been lying here, I've thought of one thing I had forgotten, a thing to make me laugh, aside from the antics of the babies, who are bigger now, of course, and who are, of course, full of antics. The thing I keep remembering is that you don't need these letters to tell you where we are, that you have had your own amazing nose all along. But, at the same time, writing to you is like ... wait ... I think ... I hear a scratching sound ... as if ... something ... Wait! ... Maybe it's Hazel coming for a visit again after all ...There it is ... a scratching sound, but ... This one is ... too loud ... somewhere above ... very near ... must check to see what it is ...

(*Let not the faint of heart proceed without trepidation.*)

JANE LETTER #34

Dear Danny,

Here's what happened the last night I wrote: I proceeded carefully to see about the scratching noise, and unfortunately, it was Double00, of course, not Hazel. I knew that raccoon had been sharing my cat food in the past, during the time when Chris and Jon used to leave some by the door, but I never knew he went any farther inside the shed or stayed here after the meals. On that last night I am telling you about, I moved in by the food dish, which was still empty ... or ... now empty ... Of course! And, in a flicker, it did occur to me that maybe Double00 had been a visitor in my area more than I knew. Who knows for how long? And he was leaving nothing in the way of food for me which is why I thought that Jon and Chris had stopped bringing any ... Well, whatever the truth is, this night I passed the empty food dish by the shed door and wound my way toward the opposite window where the noise seemed to be originating. As I turned one box corner, I came face to face with that black and brown masked face, those needle-point sharp eyes. I jumped back. Surprised also, Double00 made a sort of grunting sound as he pushed both shoulders and then all of himself between two piles of boxes, tumbling them all down and sideways. Glaring at me and blocking both food bowl and entrance way, he shook free and rose up on back legs, in a fury. I looked upwards by instinct, planning to move higher. Crouching down in this human-made, precarious cavern, I prepared to spring upward but ... I hesitated ... He can climb too. I've seen him; he's a good climber. I hesitated, only a moment, but in that tiny moment, he fell upon my crouching self; it was as if he wrapped his entire body around me like a tunnel rug, like the black cat fury on that back porch. In the middle of boxes, we tumbled sideways,

I on the bottom, desperate, claws extended, wildly seeking some stable protrusion, anything other than an empty box to push off of, to push myself out from under. He straddled on top snapping his mouth to catch any part of my face. I twisted sideways, slipping into a turn over, dislocated several cartons and pushed until finally, using just the floor boards themselves, I shot out from under. I'm smaller and I'm smooth enough, even fast ... Yes! Yes! I'm faster. I fell away, and leapt upwards. I went high, onto and over piles of crates and various other containers, around, down and behind him, back outside. I'd bet I was outside before Double00 even turned to see me, before he reached the top of the first box mountain and long before the boxes and he all fell scrambling to the floor!

Once I was back underneath the locked shed, I was relieved to find I had no desperate bite wounds. I could feel one scratch on the left ear and something near that eye. Of course, I can't see either one of these wounds, but they don't feel deep. The kittens were hungry. I cleaned up and fed them.

Then, I lay with the babies and thought about moving. No one could feel safe in or near this place anymore. I watched these little ones as they held onto me, as they fell quiet and asleep; I was still purring and with my eyes half closed, but I could see the tiny sucking movements as their mouths remembered milk, and later, some slight leg twitching as their paws caught silky dream moths.

I began to plan our move. The first job was to find another and safer place. I decided to look over on the other side of the big street, the Dead Street as I call it. I do hate that crossing, but when I think back, I think I have never seen Double00 on the other side, and I remember also a building there, very large, with space underneath.

Once more, I am hesitating to do what I have to. What if the kittens wake up and begin mewing, begin wobbling and wiggling out from under the shed, squirming this way and that, getting lost and attracting a predator, like Double00? I've been thinking possibly I should wait a day or two longer; then they will be older and larger.

Ah, but then, I realize ... then they'd likely crawl out and get lost even faster and farther.

Being a mother brings about extra uncertainty in the facing of the unknown, but extra comfort in remembering the known, like the face of you, dear Danny Lunder.

Jane

JANE LETTER #35

When finally I felt ready to leave and find a new home, I left with a purpose so important that I moved along without hesitation. I turned north by the restaurant, and only paused once briefly when I saw the Dead Street spread out in front of me; seeing it, even empty, and knowing I had to go across, brought up that tingling little sick jab in my throat. The moon showed the time to be just before sunrise. If you remember, Danny, immediately on the other side of that street, is a large building they call brick with shrubs planted close to its sides. I crept along between the bushes and the wall, and I began to notice little square openings at regular intervals on the bottom of the wall. Each had a thin wire covering, maybe to keep me out! But…pretty soon, of course, I found one whose cover had split open wide. Inside, the ground was dry, and there was an endless clean space, with sturdy posts holding things up, all underneath that building. I confirmed what I had thought earlier: that this would be a good home.

I spent a restless next day, as you can imagine. I knew I had to wait until dark to move the babies, and along with fear of Double00 returning, I began to feel hot throbbings along the side of my head, by the ear and eye; the scratch there hurt when I tried to clean it. I've been shaking my head every few minutes, but nothing changes.

Finally, the day began to end, and I became alert with decision making: Which of the four should be the first to be carried away and left alone in a strange place? Rochefort, as I've said, reminds me of CS, who is (as I'd be one to know) an independent sort, a bit wild and irresponsible but a wiry survivor. Roulade and Rotisserie are sweet little things, delicate and beautiful but … I stop a minute and give a "murrouh" for sounding so stuck in one way of thought. Why, it's as if I'd already decided that the first to go would have to be a male and strong enough to ... get a little messed up, if he had to. At that moment I thought of what Hazel would say on this subject and smiled with a little "chirrup."

But old thoughts are hard to change, I see, and I had decided without realizing it that Reuben was the best choice. For one thing, he is black and shinny, so much like the night, so easy to be hidden. For another thing, Reuben is one of those polite, easy-going creatures who never seem to fuss or bother. Where he is put down, there he sleeps—provided, of course, he's had enough to eat. His drawback, then, is being heavy, because, of the four, he has eaten the most, and although he never pushes himself forward, he always seems to eat the amount for two. I, because I have not been eating well and have no experience in carrying kittens, have to practice lifting him, getting the right hold and upswing.

I let my mouth and teeth find their way around Reuben's plump neck and arrange a nice little grip; then I did a slow careful lifting up, oh, but then a little tilting to the side, in favor of the pounding in my eye, and, sure enough, his head slid past my mouth, and all of him slipped to the ground, released. He set about locating a food source; I determined to start over. Balance was the answer. That and a firmer grip. Not a nice tender grip. A secure, stable grip. Something with authority.

After four (and I considered that to be a lucky sign) after four positionings and four liftings, I developed the proper hold and practiced a little... well, not a walk, exactly, but a gate we call "truntaling," which is faster than a walk but short of a run.

I wanted to leave before Double00 showed up, so the time to begin was at once. That meant the Dead Road would not be as empty as it is later in the night. Never mind. I knew the street, I knew the way.

Reuben was heavy and did become lopsided just before we reached the sidewalk. I put him down, shook my head and redid my mouth. I waited until the street was entirely clear of travelers. All went well, and when I released Reuben easy onto the ground under the building, he moved only his rear paws an inch or two before he tucked his head under them and went back to sleep.

After Reuben, what a relief it was to carry little Roulade, swinging, light and sleepy, as we went. I placed her carefully next to Reuben and waited a moment to see them snuggle up together, to watch her give him two licks behind one ear with her eyes closed.

I returned to the restaurant and saw that Chris and Jon had brought the nightly food; it was in its usual place, and I should have been in my usual state of hunger. But when my nose went to the edge of the bowl, it told me not to eat, and even though everything in the vicinity seemed normal enough, I found myself moving away, licking my nose, trying to stimulate good smells, I suppose. Then back under the smaller shed, I found Roquefort halfway out of the wooden flap, his head stuck in between that and the ground and pitiful little squeaks sliding from the compressed side of his mouth. Well, that decided who would be next in line to head out.

Of course, if there was going to be trouble, it would be caused by Roquefort. And there was, and it was. He is a squirmer, has been all along, and I knew that, but really, what could I have done differently? Left him behind? If I repositioned him once, I did it seven times or more, before we even got to the Dead Road. Once there, I stopped to consider. Better get him straight before starting the cross because, of course, the worst time to reposition would be in the middle of that street. And it was. Halfway across, Roquefort flipped himself almost completely upside down, and squealing as he went over, sprawled—legs flat out—on his stomach, in the street. I opened my mouth to grab his rowdy neck, and he turned back, feet up, buffing a front paw-hold on my face, and doing the rabbit kick to my neck. I hollered out in pain then for myself, for my head was stretched tight with it, and I could feel that pain trying to escape too, streaking down into my front legs. Still, there was Roquefort, holding on and puntering for all he was worth. Jumbling backwards, I looked up to see the car only a street block's length away. I stood stiff; for a second, I didn't move, then I fell sideways half on top of Roquefort and reaching here and there for any part of him to hold onto, but he, in typical kitten fashion, thought I'd taken up his game and went more seriously into his practice of new mauling techniques. I looked up again in horror, crying out, then grabbing the first solid protrusion that touched my mouth, I yanked that incorrigible kitten, by the tail, toward the curb ... as the car swerved to miss us, just barely. I closed my eyes and thought, "just as barely" as it had once swerved on purpose to hit Jake, in a time that now seems so long ago.

When I picked him up finally, again—with a viselike grip this time—I was angry enough to SHAKE the life out of that kitten, and I did move more roughly than was necessary the rest of the way. And he did keep on squirming and squealing the rest of the way. So, when we got to the new home, that Roquefort wildness woke up everybody else, all were then squirming and squealing, and nothing would do but to feed all three. Well, I was growing more and more impatient to get back and bring home Rotisserie, so I was slow to relax for feeding, and, afterwards, though I was even more anxious to return and finish the move, I could hardly lift my body to stand when it was time to go.

I found Rotisserie, sitting there in the middle of what used to be her home, repeating identical plaintive mews, one little noise after another. She wanted to eat too, and although I tried to explain why we had to move on, I could tell she didn't understand. I'll be glad when these little ones learn to listen.

Now, this next morning finds us all here together. And even my head feels a bit lighter as if it were somehow floating free, drifting, and I do hope that means the wound is healing. In the meantime, the air is also lighter, with a new warmth, new bird songs and the reassuring sounds of humans laughing somewhere out along the sidewalks.

And so we wait for you with new hope,
Jane

JANE LETTER #36

Danny, I tell you, my thoughts ... and first I tell you they pass in and around my head without stopping long enough to be known clearly. Sometimes, I can feel being in some other place with you, with everyone together, somewhere gentle it seems ... a grass- and flower-covered field. I can see it ... billowing outward like an old quilt, shaken slowly, full of early morning colors—pinks and yellows—and a soft light green just beginning to rub against us and drift on toward the horizon; the kittens are sleeping between your legs ... Then, I open my eyes, wanting to be in that field ... and then ... I do rise up and drift and land as softly as a dandelion seed; I see everything, and all is well, all well, at last.

I know there were the things we expected ... what were they? Homes, I think, and friends. And some we never expected, that turned out for our good fortune and some that did not ... and some that changed ... though strangely, not my name. And that I don't know why. But even if my name had changed and even if all the adventures had been different, there'd still be you who wouldn't change and others like Jake or Hazel or Tom or even my lost sister Boots, not to mention poets like Maisie, all those who'd come in and out, changing or not, but would always be held close even after only a brief stay, maybe a saving stay, all held in the heart, expected or not .

> And so I will sign my letter, holding you as close as you always are, and with the same love as we always had, and I will take this letter back to be with the others at the "No Loitering" restaurant ... where you will find it and you will come to find us.
> Jane

BOOK II

Part Three

In which Danny covers a lot of ground right up to the end.

When Danny arrived finally at the restaurant with the No Loitering sign, after following old scents and many dead ends, cold scents, and Jane's directions, he found the latest letters. His mouth was entirely full of letters by now, but the ground was full of new scents also and his body, from nose to thrashing tail, was full of an excitement difficult to control. He put the letters down and began an almost frantic back and forth, somewhat circular, investigation of the area. He found all fresh information about Jane and more connected, related new scents. He appeared to be everywhere at once.

The two humans didn't arrive in time to see Danny disappear beside the small shed; they didn't seem to hear him digging and thumping around under the side of the shed, but he saw them as soon as he was finished and carrying the last letters out to the back door. One human was on a ladder with his hands holding onto and trying to unhook that squeaking old sign while the other stood at the bottom trying to hold still a rotten old ladder.

The bark just exploded from Danny's throat. The letters spayed from his mouth. Maybe he could smell the illness on the last letters or on the ground, and so maybe he felt anxious, excited, and alarmed in general.

(Danny tells me I should have guessed that it was all of the above. E.T.)

For several reasons then, he barked and continued to bark as he took off down the side of the restaurant, to the front, then came back, then ran off again. Finally, he stopped below the ladder and just barked without pause.

"That dog is barking," said one of the boys.

"What makes you say that," said the other.

"This is a Lassie moment, Jon."

"You mean …?"

"I do."

"Right."

Danny remembers gathering the letters and running, the letters locked in his jaws, although some may have dropped off on the way; he remembers hearing the humans behind him calling out, "Good boy," "Good dog," and "On, you Husky"—the way people do, although the last one did not ring a bell for him. But most of all, he remembers the moment he reached the little open vent and scented Jane inside and knew she was there and knew she was ill. He barked with renewed vigor, in despair and need.

Jane pulled herself outside and raised her head to his: "Danny Lunder! What a wonder! I knew you would be here soon!"

Danny remembers licking her head and whatever else his tongue came near, and as the kittens came staggering from the opening, lopsiding all over the place, he found himself licking their hissing heads and their bodies too, in no particular order, even randomly knocking them down to get at their stomachs, then back to Jane until she lowered her head, tired of the effort even happiness took.

As he licked, Danny vaguely remembers human voices going on, then a car driving up and a young woman getting out, all the voices low, on and on, and at some point the word "vet," which both disturbed and encouraged him.

He remembers everyone being gathered into the car. First Jane, removed from his tongue and lifted carefully into a box, without any protest (which seemed to him a bad sign). But, he thought vaguely, it has to be. The boys held the squealing kittens pretty well. Then he, Danny, gathering up his letters, climbing into the back seat, hiding the letters on the floor, under the seat, while nobody noticed, then trying to lick Jane some more. Finally, the one called Jon got in the back seat, shut the door, cushioned Danny's head away from Jane, and the car moved—moved and stopped, as they do, until Jane was left, at the vet. Danny assumed. The kittens continued squealing all the way.

Soon enough, the car stopped one last time, for good, beside an old house with nothing but trees and grass in front of it as far as Danny could see, and they led him to the back where the yard was fenced in but still very large to circle the house. He was let go on the back door porch; the kittens were taken inside. He stood at the door that led to the inside and waited for the kittens. He must have been crying because someone kept saying, "It's all right, boy. They'll have a little supper and be right out." And someone brought him a meal too, although he'd be hard pressed to remember exactly what it was. No matter. He ate it in one gulp or nearly.

He waited some more and then there they were! Right out! Needing their mouths wiped, tasting of canned something, throwing themselves this way and that, off in all directions and covered with Jane's merry scent, especially the little gray and cloudy one that looked like Jane. Or was that just his wish? He had a time getting them clean and keeping them in order; they crawled up his ears and tried to pin down his tail, over and over; then, one by one their eyes closed and they fell asleep wherever they happened to be at the time: between his legs, half under his belly and beside his head.

As he placed his head carefully down between two kittens, Danny heard the people talking some more:

"I can't believe it."

"Never saw such a thing."

"If anyone told me, I wouldn't believe it."

A pause, after which all three people spoke together:

"Do you think ... do you ... could they ... think they know ... how could they ... know each other ... or maybe knew ... even before?"

"Why not?"

Everyone laughed.

Life in the "farm house," as the humans called it, was wonderful for an animal, and even better for five!

It was not that Danny forgot about Jane; no, no. He expected her each day; he might be patrolling the fish pond or the back gate and stop still, head up and tilted sideways; he'd listen and sniff the air and know she was missing.

And he knew immediately when she had returned.

THE FINAL LETTER

Dear mother of Jane or, as Jane has called you, Mahrowh,

I hope you will excuse the liberty I take of writing to you. I who am a stranger to you am a great friend of your kitten, now cat, Jane. I know we can never be too sure you will read any of her letters to you in their original form as directly from Jane, but some day maybe you will pick up this little book to remember her time with you and discover the events of her later life and her lucky good fortune.

Because we are making this book as a surprise for Jane herself, we decided not to ask her to write you the final letter, but Ms. Throckmorton and I feel you would want to know what a fine spot we have fallen into, by luck and by kindness, the place we now presume to call home: It has rugs to go under and stairs to go up, around, and down, radiators with warm covers to lie on (not for me, Danny Lunder, you know; I am thinking of the cats now.) and little doors to go in and out of. Once outside, it has grass to chew on, trees to go up and down and around, bushes to go under, even if you're only pretending to be afraid. And in all of these places, we find crawling, wiggling, hopping creatures to play with and not to have to eat. We even find some creatures that, after experimentation or word of mouth, we won't even play with, much less eat.

> *(I am reminded of Jane when I say: we learn from all our experiences in life, and one thing I have learned from my editing job here is that no matter how friendly and close one may feel toward her employer, or however good her advice and knowledge may be, one must never expect to gain full acceptance as an equal if one is an insect and her employer is a mammal. The best one can hope for is a kind of distant respect on both sides, the key word here being "distant." It is a good lesson for me; it is, as Danny Lunder might want to say, a giant step toward understanding and accepting my place in the world and in giving direction toward future job searches. But so be it as far as being an insect is concerned. E.T.)*

If you are reading this volume, Mah, you will already be familiar with Jane's earlier adventures and so on. For that reason, I will limit my topics to the time after she had her kittens and finished writing the letters here to you and me, after I found her and she was ill and had to go to the vet.

When our humans brought Jane back from the vet, she was feeling better, but she had been sick unto death, and no one wanted me to lick her. She stayed in a carrier cage, one of the many unknowns she had come to know during her illness, including: what illness means, what different cages mean, how the vet, and shots fit in—much that we had spoken of when she was a kitten, much that comes to all of us in time. As she recovered, I would lie with my nose on the metal cage door; she would lie inside with her nose inside the door, and we discussed these things.

Our three humans, called Meg, Jon, and Chris, have become to be like the old Master to me, only better, being three! They are also more loving on all counts, being three, touching me whenever they pass by and telling me I am a hero all the time. So, I believed them when they said, "Jane will get well if we let her rest and sleep." They told me I could lick her as soon as she got better. They told me I was a good dog.

And so, in a few days she came out of the carrier and we spent some quiet time in the house library. How long is unclear. I may have mentioned in earlier pages how unreliable time became for me either when I was upset or unusually happy; well, that's the way it was then. It seemed my only desire was to wash her all over, like new. One afternoon she stood up, a little wobbly, and rubbed against my mouth and eyes and then, of all things, then she licked me! Jane did! I'd never felt her tongue before. She licked my whole face, and I finally discovered what that rough, sturdy tongue meant, the tongue she had told me about, the strong cat tongue like yours when you took care of her and Boots. I know now how very much loving its roughness sends.

After a few more days, Meg let the kittens come in to visit their Mom. None but the little gray one seemed to recognize her. I said it was because of the vet scent still all around the cage, such an unnatural thing to smell, and then too, I reminded Jane that she had changed; she was more … relaxed than I remembered. Well, for whatever reason, coming into the library, the kittens acted like fools, with feeble little hissings and bared teeth, pitiful little tuffs of short fur going up along the spines as they came near the cage.

Jane watched as the kittens backed away, then fell all over each other in confusion. I stood in the middle and tried not to bark but to grunt a kind of reasoned encouragement. Then, the one little gray kitten separated, paying no attention to all the others' hissings and such; she sniffed the cage, and after she and Jane briefly touched noses, I noticed that Jane gave her some perfunctory licks on the ear. After a short moment, our friend Meg gathered them all up and took them out to the kitchen. I wish I could carry them that way, all at one time.

Now she's recovered, and her babies are older, and even if she missed most of their growing up, Jane doesn't seem to notice much what the kittens do; they're on their own now, I guess. Oh, she will give them a lick or two and a bump or so, and a paw buff if they get rowdy. Generally, she spends her time lying on the back porch, front feet over the edge, purring and curling her toes in and out, watching a day bounce around on its own, too. Yep, she seems happy enough just to watch. She says everything will go up and down or it won't. She doesn't hide from or jump upon me very much anymore, no more than she looks very much at the past.

Well, as she has said in letters to us both, what one expects does not always come about (or what one wishes either, of course), but then, she says, sometimes, it does. And she looks at me and bumps my chin, so very peacefully.

(I know Danny Lunder had wanted, or expected, me to become more friendly with Jane in the beginning of our project because he thought if I got to know her I would understand her better which, in turn, would enrich my understanding of our narrative. One night he persuaded me to travel incognito out to the porch to, if not meet Jane and her family, at least observe them. We left the library at 8 P.M. so that we would be back before 10 at which the time the humans always

255

shut the door, and I always began my work. On the night in question, as he instructed, I crawled up onto Danny's head and into his ear and hid myself there behind the natural Lab protection flap that comes down over the opening. When we reached the porch, Danny gave the three-bark signal we had agreed on, whereupon I pulled aside the protection flap and carefully looked out. I saw the large, gray cat, along with the four smaller ones, all leaping into the air, 10 legs extended, 50 claws expanded and a bright white moon moth floating just barely above them, out of reach. But although the night air was soft and the moth's escaping wings waved like fairy boat sails, I backed quickly away; I backed so far into the rear of Danny's ear that he gave a violent head shake; he kept on shaking as I kicked with all six feet to remind him to take me back to the library without delay.. E.T.)

Now, to bring you up to the present: It's springtime again, with a sunset of hazy pink promise and a dapper breeze; almost a human year has passed, and our work on this book of letters is finished, except for one last section, which E.T. will type as soon as the library door is closed. We have managed to keep our work a secret so far, but the excitement is huge.

Meanwhile, we are happy together. The kittens are almost grown and still here. People have come to take them away, but have never left with one. From what I heard, our humans could not agree as to which kitten should leave. From what I heard, they could not agree which kitten should take a chance on having the same thing happen to it that had happened to Jane and me. Although they weren't sure what that was. Soon, they will read this book and know everything!

As for the original letters, I have kept most and still carry them around from time to time. Their scents remind me of the past. I like to remember back then. Jane, of course, does not, and reminds me often enough that, for her, memories of the past are not worth much more than yesterday's dog kibble, especially when they have become as soggy and shredded as those I carry around. She says I might just put them out in the sun to dry up and blow away. So, as the humans say, "We will have to agree to disagree on that point."

If you should ever read our book, please be sure to know that we thank you so much for having Jane and we hope you have also a pleasing and comfortable life.

Yours truly from us: Danny Lunder, Edith Throckmorton (and Jane)

EPILOGUE

(Deaeer REaeder. I   cannn nott find E.T. anywhere   I   ave
looked   bbbubut

Do remember
she spoke of   tthe larger markets in ///??? once she fouuunde
success and recognition withth the publishing of these letters.
Maybe   didn't wait. If so,,, I myself, Dannylunder, amm
nnooww   tytuping what sje calllled te eppeiglogue without
help.

ToOO bad I don't know about editing words I hav todo the bestyt
i can and my paws are deffinfitty toooo larggesh for this work
buut since this bok is ment tp be a surprise to Jane I do not whant
to show ahead of time. III willl waits   to seeee If E.T commes ouit
ronnitgh, D.L.)

Latrter;
           E.T. neverr   came oput to eat thaatnite last weekk   i
Ilook all over froher and tthijk SShhe must ber in SOAm   boxc
headdder fort New York assshe sAiD jobbbs therrr werre good
ford eeidditors
           I   hartrt hataae hate this quwrk   my pawews ttooo
bbig   suse use one nale…
           Thissis the e end tthen. . so

           Asas I said   NO I don"t minmnd the past. Some say

259

thehy woudkjld change it tobeeee aaalllgood, but I don't tink I
would. NOOO   butt I do say I'm gladf

        thihngs
        turned out allll rightt foooorus for now aaat lest last
lleast

        annd I hopoe   will   forrr you, derear readder also.

                    If   nnno t   yet,   ther will   beet
good   foor yyyyou
sooooon.,..

wood be   so glad   for us   whern thjat hasppens !

            Fffor noww, With besttte regards and d f ond
        memories I am your hooopplfulleyy nw new frend,
        DANNNyLunder

            Thhhee ENDF

ACKNOWLEDGEMENTS

Bette and Rick, I was going to say this book could never have been written without your help, but, of course, I realized at once that it surely could have been written without your help, somehow, to some extent maybe, but then it would have been no fun at all, only constant uncertainty, headache and stress, ending, I fear, without any of the resulting love and kindness that Danny Lunder and Jane, and perhaps even Edith Throckmorton, would have wanted.

THANK YOU!

ABOUT THE AUTHOR

Barbara Hite, former high school and college teacher, has written extensively for the theater. Her play "Sissy and the Baby Jesus" won the Stanley Drama Award in 1981. *LETTERS from Jane* was inspired by her work with Cat Rescue in Norfolk, Virginia, where she lives with husband, Rick, illustrator of *JANE*.